FOR SENIORS AND THOSE WHO WILL BE SENIORS...

THE MOORE THE MERRIER

By Jean Anderson Moore

(with lots of help)

ISBN:1461020034
ISBN-13:9781461020035

DEDICATION

To Bob, my beloved husband of 56 years,

And to our lovely daughters, Karen and Pam,

who have put up with my craziness,

And especially to our son David,

who read, edited, and graded all these stories

that allowed me to fulfill my senior bucket list.

I love ya'll

CONTENTS

Thanks for the Memories...Wherever They Are

PREFACE TO LAUGHTER

I have always loved to laugh, especially when there are others around to laugh with me. I took a class about humor that concluded that a big hard belly laugh every day is one of the most healthy things you can do for yourself. Life is hard; you're born, you work, and then you die. If you can't laugh about the things that happen along that road, life becomes a real drag. Love, of course, gives us the strength to overcome much of life's diversities. Love makes the world go round, but laughter keeps us from getting dizzy.

Humor may have helped preserve the species in prehistoric times. Although realism saved cave men and women from being gobbled by tigers, without an optimistic sense of humor and adventure, they would never have ventured away from the cave in the first place. If they needed a laugh they could always turn their animal skin coats inside out and the fur against their skin would tickle their fancy.

The *Bible* tell us, "A merry heart doeth good like a medicine." (Proverbs 17:22) We all know that God has a sense of humor. Just look at animals like the duck-billed platypus and the hedge-hog.

I know animals have a sense of humor. Our family was in Washington DC and paid an early morning visit to the zoo. In the elephant enclosure they were just filling the pool. One of the elephants discovered that if he held his trunk over the pipe of water running into the pool, he could squirt the humans that were walking by the the enclosure, and make them squeal and run. He knew exactly what he was doing and he repeated the joke every time a new group of victims came down the path. He was getting his elephant jollies.

Dr. Norman Cousins who wrote *Healing Power of Laughter*, laughed so hard at the Marx Brothers movies that he was able to have several hours of pain free rest. He laughed himself back to health. He felt that the significant thing about laughter is it provides internal exercise...a form of jogging for the innards. Laughter boosts endorphins that are the body's natural pain killers.

When I ask my computer about the healing power of laughter, it gave me five pages of references to read. Scientific evidence has shown that laughter helps people breathe easier and it massages the heart and other vital organs. Laughter burns calories...up to 20% more than walking. With as much laughing as I do, I should be 20% thinner. It may also increase the release of disease-fighting cells in the immune system. Like exercise, laughter quickens the pulse and stimulates the cardiovascular system. In experiments, students who watched funny movies were found to have an increased flow of infection-fighting proteins in their saliva, so laugh out loud before you play kissy face.

I had a dear friend who volunteered with me at the Genealogy Library. She arrived one day with the shocking revelation that she had breast cancer. We were devastated because she was so young,. There wasn't much I could do medically, but I made it my goal to make her laugh out loud. I found jokes, funny stories, and humorous situations, and I'd pass them on to her and we'd have a good laugh together. Well, she was a real trooper. She went through lumpectomy, chemo, and then radiation, and she didn't miss a single shift at the library. I like to think I helped, but she was the one who had the sense of humor and laughed out loud. Laughter is the shortest distance between two people and in addition to its healing effects, we became good friends.

So my purpose in putting this book together for you, my dear friends, is so we can share a smile and a laugh at everyday experiences.   Remember the adage, live well, love much, and *laugh often.*

Becoming a Senior...

It's a long, hard road to become a senior, but when you consider the alternative, you better enjoy the journey.

IN THE BEGINNING

I don't want to give the impression that I just became funny in my senior years. Oh no, I have been funny all my life, but I started seriously writing our humorous adventures after Bob and I retired in 1994. We had lived in Cedar City, Utah where Bob was a university professor, and I taught in grade school. We raised our three children: Karen who produces musical magic, David who is a word wizard, and Pamela who turns scraps of paper into awesome art. They had given us eight beautiful grandchildren, but none of them were living in Cedar City. When retirement began to stare us in the face, we made a *bucket list* of things we wanted to do before we *kicked the bucket.* Number one on our list was to move close to our family who lived in Salt Lake City. We planned to bug the heck out of them just to get even.

So in 1992, we bought an acre of land in Highland, just south of Salt Lake. We pulled a trailer onto the lot, had it hooked up to electricity and we were in business. We moved into our trailer during that summer and started chopping weeds and planting small trees. We bought 100 Austrian pines and 100 poplars, and planted them in one spot where we could keep them watered. In the fall we headed back down south to school.

The next summer we came back to our little trailer to build a big garage/shop complete with a bathroom. The size of this building made some of our neighbors nervous. They weren't sure what we had planned, and an acre of land required a big home, so I took a can of spray paint and wrote, "This is a garage" on the side of the building. It was eventually covered with bricks, but for the time being the neighbors were much friendlier, and relieved that we weren't building small low-income houses on our property.

In May 1994, we sold our condo in Cedar City, and retired from our teaching jobs. My last day at school I wore a sign around my neck, "I'm an orphan, I'm homeless, and I'm out of work." The sixth graders at school took up a collection for me, and gave me 11 cents and a button. We bid a sad farewell to our friends and neighbors we had loved for twenty-five years, and headed north with our last load of household goods and a coop of chickens tied on top of the truck.

That summer was a beehive of activity. Building a new house was #2 on our *bucket list*. Bob had spent two years designing this home. They say a marriage that can survive building a house, can survive anything, so we tried to work together without killing each other. I decorated the inside of the house and he did the outside and yard. David and Bob surrounded our acre with a white vinyl fence and transplanted all 200 trees around the perimeter. Builder Bob turned the finished garage into a workshop by setting up the woodworking tools that he had accumulated, and it morphed into the control center of all the activities. The workmen and the neighbors could always find a phone, a bathroom, and a popsicle there. I kept busy refinishing furniture and organizing the stuff in Bob's workshop. My need to organize always drives him crazy, but I promised not to throw out anything unless I asked his permission. And I kept that promise, sometimes. One afternoon a painter came in and found me in a cloud of sawdust and looked over my projects. He offered to spray paint my antique dresser, my folding table and my nine pieces of wrought iron patio furniture. It took him a half hour to paint everything that would have taken me weeks. I gave him extra popsicles the rest of the week.

By September we were all ready to move in, except for the bathrooms, so for a few days we lived in our new house but had to run out to the shop when nature called. It took us another year to put in the landscaping and sprinklers, with a lot of help from family and friends, and we planted 30 fruit trees and a big garden. When we turned the irrigation water onto the lot, we could float our canoe in the west end. The grandkids would jump in and pretend they were sailing into the sunset on a foot of water. We had a big fire pit and spent many hours cooking and playing games with family and friends in that big yard. It was a great place, but a lot of work! My knees and Bob's back lasted for ten years, until on our way to Salt Lake one day, we saw some beautiful condos in a gated community in Draper. We sold our home to a couple with younger bodies and began leisure condo living.

BUCKET LIST #3 – RAISE HORSES

Now picture this; a nice house with an acre of grass and trees, and two old duffers with nothing to do but ride around on a lawnmower, plant flowers and pull weeds. This was the perfect time to work on #3 on our bucket list. Ever since I read *National Velvet* I've wanted a horse, but big horses scare me. Bob, however, was perfectly at ease around horses as a kid, and even had his own little colt.

We found the perfect answer for both of us. Living just down the street was a young lady, Tori, who had a farm full of pets, including registered miniature horses. They are not ponies; think smaller, like the size of a great Dane. There they were, lovable mini-horses. They were beautiful, gentle, and intelligent, and just the right size for me and our little grandchildren. Bob came home and measured off space for stables and a small barn with storage for hay, and he was building again. We named our place Highland Haven Miniatures and we were in business.

Tori helped us choose our first little filly; gray with a black mane and tail. Pride and Joy, or PJ, was just a baby when we moved her to our farm. Horses are very social, and we knew she wouldn't be alone long, but I worried about her, and tried to keep her company as much as I could those first few days. PJ had lots of visitors in the daytime, with all the grandchildren and neighbors. But the first night it snowed, the silly horse stood out by the fence watching the back door, and she wouldn't go into her stall. The snow was accumulating on her back and I made a frantic late night call to Tori. "What shall I do? Shall I go put a blanket on her? Shall I bring her in our garage?"

Tori said, "For heaven's sake settle down, Jean. She's a horse and she'll be just fine. Now go to bed!" But I spent most of the night watching my little horse from the bedroom window.

PJ loved to be scratched, and if I sat on a bucket, she would back up to me and try to sit on my lap like a big old lap dog. We had to stop that when she sat down and we collapsed, bucket and all.

She watched Bob cleaning the stalls by shoveling the manure into a bucket. One day she carefully backed up to the bucket and made a manure deposit of her own. Minis can actually be housebroken, but we didn't want their little hoof prints on our new carpet. However, we did let them have the run of the yard every afternoon, and they loved that time. People would come by and bring them carrots and apples, and they obliged the visitors by being cuter than heck.

Bob and I decided early on, that raising show horses was not for us. We liked raising the babies, so we had many horses move in and out of our farm, because they had to pay for their keep by reproducing. We bought Niki from a breeder in California because of her good bloodlines, but she was a quirky little filly. She bonded with Bob and he was hers and hers alone, and she didn't have much to do with the other horses or humans on the farm. It was difficult breeding her, but when she did finally have a little filly, she would only let Bob into her stall. He picked up the baby and then had to stand between Niki and me as I put iodine on the baby's umbilical. Niki was outraged that I would get near her baby, and she tried to push past Bob to get at me.

Niki loved everything about Bob, and when he was bent over a shovel she would often grab his cap off his head and wave it at him, until he grabbed it back. But when she wanted food she could be very sweet. She loved to mooch when we were having lunch in the back yard. She would lay her chin on the picnic table and whinny until some sympathetic soul would give her a snack. Doughnut holes were her favorite, but she also accepted fruit and potato chips and anything else we offered.

Brownie, one of our favorite little mares, loved the fruit on our trees when it was in season. She would reach up, grab a branch and back up until she pulled it right off the tree, and then she'd feast. She'd climb up into the rock planter so she could munch on the grapes and the leaves. She was also fond of bird seed, and would tip the bird feeders over and lick them clean. Brownie gave us six beautiful babies, and she was a good mother. She also loved to be groomed, and that was my job. I'd sing, and brush her mane and tail, and Brownie would stand there as long as I did. I really think she enjoyed the cowboy songs I'd sing. I frequently forgot the words and made up my own, but Brownie didn't care as long as I had a brush in my hand.

Our favorite horse was Gold, our palomino stallion. He was judged Reserve Grand Champion in Utah County and was beautiful and studly, and he knew it. Before the traffic got too bad on our street, we used to walk the horses around Highland, and Gold would call out to all the mares in the pastures, and they would gallop over to the fence to see the animal that sounded like a horse, but was the size of a dog. He would always prance around and swish his tail for the girls. There was one field that had a little calf in it, and when Gold trotted over and stuck his nose in the fence, the calf licked his face. Gold didn't like that and he rared back tossing Bob against the rocks into a ditch. This gave Bob some pretty colorful bruises on his left side, and it also gave him an idea. He could take pictures of the bruises and claim wife abuse, then sue me for my social security checks. Yeah, right! Gold fathered many beautiful babies in and around Utah County, including our little PJ. He pulled a cart in parades and gave rides to kids during county fairs.

One day when Bob was away, Gold got stuck between his fence and the side of his stall. He was frightened and so was I. I went out and grabbed his tail, yelled "back," a command he knew and I pulled on his tail as hard as I could. He came back a few steps and then forward again, but I kept the pressure on his tail. It took me about fifteen minutes of pulling and yelling until his flanks came free and he knew he could back out. I sat down on the grass shaking and exhausted. Gold ran over and got a drink and then chuffed at me for sitting in his stall, the ingrate.

We took the horses and their babies around to visit schools and assisted living facilities. People loved to feed and pet the them. One little guy was reluctant to touch a horse, but stayed outside after the other kids had gone in. I said, "Would you like to pet Brownie?" He didn't say anything, but he walked up and laid his check against her flank.

We took Gold and his cart to a horse parade in Lehi and a man wanted to buy everything, and offered us a price we could not refuse. When he came to the farm to get Gold, he saw Niki and offered to buy her also. At the same parade a lady saw Brownie and her baby Cinnamon and bought both of them. That left us with two little stallions, and that does not make for good breeding, so we sold them and within a month we were out of the horse business. We've almost forgotten all the work they were, but we'll always have ten years of wonderful memories of those precious little creatures.

CREATION OF ELDER HONEY

The year 1999 the entire family gathered at Highland Haven to celebrate the holidays. January 1, 2000 came, the world did not end as some predicted. We all stood out on our front porch to see the partial solar eclipse. We did look a little silly with our heavy coats over our pajamas, as we watched the sun through our thick welding glasses.

That summer Karen and Bobby's oldest son, Rob was called on a mission for the LDS Church to Ukraine. He was to report to the Missionary Training Center (MTC) with bag and baggage accompanied by various assorted family members on a Wednesday. So off we went, with Bob and I tagging along. When you walk in the door there is a plethora of volunteers to meet and greet the families and tell them where to go. After the missionaries pick up packets of information, get an orange *dork* dot stuck on their shirts to indicate they are new missionaries, they go with their entourage into a big room where they meet the MTC mission president and his wife. They are shown a great film about missions throughout the world. Then they kiss their families good bye, and the missionaries go out one door and with tears in their eyes, the teary eyed families go out the other door to the parking lot. It was a memorable event and Bob and I could sense a special spirit about that place.

The next day we called the MTC to volunteer our services on Wednesdays. After all, it was only about a forty-five minute drive from Highland. "That's so nice of you," the lady said, "But most of these people have been doing this for years, and we have a long waiting list of volunteer wannna-bes. However, we do have a need for full time missionaries to serve in the Language

Interpretation Office. Would you be interested in serving a full time mission here at the MTC?"

"Well we don't speak any languages except English, unless you include pig Latin," sez I, trying to be funny. She explained that we would be working in an office with seven other missionaries, and our job was to find interpreters for all the incoming missionaries who did not speak English. Most important for us was that we could live in our own home. Serving a mission together was on our bucket list, but it was hard to go away and leave the horses. This was perfect! So we put in our papers and within a month we were Elder and Sister Moore, MTC missionaries.

Our interpreters would meet the new people at the door of the MTC and stay with them as they went through orientation. We also furnished interpreters for their Sunday meetings and the Tuesday night devotionals. The office had compiled long lists of people who spoke twenty seven different languages. They were all volunteers also. It's amazing the amount of talented people available if you know where to look.

Bob became the supervising elder for our department, and one afternoon when things were slow, my friend Sister Pagan and I asked if we could go over to the genealogy library at BYU for a couple of hours. He gave us permission to go reluctantly, but cautioned us not to be gone too long. "Thanks, honey," I said as I headed out the door.

"That's Elder Honey to you," he quipped back at me. From then on we called him Elder Honey. Alyse, our oldest grand daughter asked her mother who Elder Honey was and why Gram kept writing all that stuff about him. Karen said, "That's Elder Grandpa Honey to you, dear."

One of our favorite missionaries was Elder B from Sicily, who loved to come into our office and give his opinions. "My mission call is to Ogden, Utah. What kind of a place is Ogden for a nice boy like me? I want to hear from an authority."

Elder Honey said, "You did hear from an authority. That's where you got your call. Besides, people in Ogden love Sicilians."

A few months after Elder B had been out, he wrote us a letter. "I love Ogden! It's the best mission ever. Everybody honks and waves at us and takes us out to eat." He even returned to Ogden after his mission was over and attended Weber State College.

Many of our missionaries wanted to live in America after their service. Some even immigrated to our home in Highland. The first was Natasha from Ukraine. She served in the Ukraine and then came to Utah on a visitors visa. She had been interpreting Russian and came into our office in tears one day. The people where she lived were going on a mission themselves and she didn't have anywhere to stay. Because of her visa, she couldn't work but she could go to school. I don't know how they expect people to go to school and not work, but that was the deal. Soft hearted Elder Honey invited her to move in with us. She stayed about 18 months and then married, and that took care of her visa problem.

About this same time, Rob was released from his mission and wanted to go to BYU, so we opened the door and let him in too. He was great with the horses, and he kept the refrigerator cleaned out by eating all the left-overs. He still does that when he comes to visit. He lived with us for about three years, and he and his friends helped us move to Draper.

Then came a beautiful young lady from Bosnia. Edlira had graduated from college, but BYU offered her a scholarship for a master's degree and a part time job. She had trouble getting a visa, however. "I'm a good person. Why can't I come to your county?" she wrote. She went home for a year, and finally went to Greece to get her visa. She was a great help with the housework, and took right over if she saw me scrubbing or cleaning.

Lera was also from the Ukraine, and she moved in and immediately got a job at the grocery store as a bag lady. She had plenty of spending money and loved to play. Her favorite place was Las Vegas. She thought all America should look like that. She finally moved to Chicago to make her fortune and we lost track of her. I guess she can find us again if she needs a place to stay.

Even Pam, her husband and three girls came to Highland for a couple of months while their new home was being finished.

Heidi, Rob's sister lived with us for a while after we were in Draper. We used to hide Subway sandwiches and drinks in our purses and smuggle them into the movie so we wouldn't have to buy expensive theater food. After six months, her parents decided she needed to come back home to Texas and get a job.

Now days we have a couple of college grand daughters that come and stay in the summer.

From Natasha's stay to this day we have not been *empty nesters* again. In church they ask if someone would like to take in some high school exchange students for a year. Elder Honey said, "Don't you dare raise your hand!" So I sat on them. They were cold anyway.

CHUB AND OTHER MOUNTAIN MOOCHES

When you build a cabin in the mountains, you have to accept the fact that you are living with a bunch of critters that love to mooch, and you better be prepared for company. First came the mice. They moved into the logs that we were using to build our mountain home. The logs were in piles by the foundation, and when we came to the bottom log, a mother mouse with four hairless little babies attached to teats, scurried right over and disappeared into the next log pile without even losing a single baby. Such tenacity!

The deer preferred to make early morning visits, to see if there were any tasty greens that had been newly planted, and they found plenty. They couldn't resist nibbling the green leaves off of our new fruit trees. To discourage them we put tubes of chicken wire around the trees until they were tall enough that the deer couldn't reach them. As the cabin went up, the regal deer still hung around even during hunting season. I encouraged them to stay near us because our area was a *no hunting* zone. I yelled at the hunters who came into our area, and hoped they wouldn't shoot at a little old lady in an orange vest.

Our porch became an observation platform where we could sit and watch the hawks riding the thermals in the sky, and an occasional owl that would silently glide past in the evenings. After our cabin was finished we drove in one day to find a couple of skunks up underneath. We weren't sure if they were living there but we gave them a wide berth as we sneaked in the back door, and then we stamped around inside, yelling and making scary noises. The next day the skunks had found a quieter place to live, thank goodness.

We hung several bird feeders around our porch to attract mooching hummingbirds, and they soon became so numerous we were afraid we might get spiked in the head as they flitted back and forth in a feeding frenzy. Gradually they became tame enough that they would sit on our finger to feed, except for one little guy we named "the Enforcer." He was very aggressive and appointed himself guardian of the feeders. He would sit at the edge of the porch, fluff himself up as big as possible, and chase off the other birds as they came to eat. The other hummers would fly acrobatic displays by swooping up and down in giant circles. This was more of a mating ritual than a protective show and one of the hummers was kind enough to built a tiny nest of spider webs and down in the lower branches of our pine tree. She raised two little babies. They were so tight in the nest that they could hardly move, but they managed to grow, and finally took off never to return. I kept the nest.

One morning a hummer flew into a window and crashed down to our porch. I thought he was dead for sure, so I put him in a chair, and went inside to get a box to bury him. But when I came back and picked him up, he began to flutter around, and giving me a dirty look, he flew home to tell his wife about the ugly giant who tried to catch him. I saw him flying around the cabin the next day, looking into the windows so he could show me how tough he was.

However, in the pecking order of mooches, squirrels are at the top of the list. In fact, the top is where we first saw Chub. We came to the cabin one spring morning, and there at the very top of a juniper tree sat Chub, hanging like a abandoned Christmas tree ornament, swaying back and forth in the breeze. That evening as we ate dinner on the porch, who should show up for a freebie, but a team of chipmunks and Chub. After chasing off the chipmunks and chowing down on our left overs, Chub disappeared into a hole under the cabin. Better him than the skunks. In the days when we were in residence, Chub would saunter up to our chairs on the porch, put his paws on our legs and stare at us with those big black eyes to see what we had to offer. We would leave him choice pieces from our salads, and he liked everything except the broccoli. It would lay on the porch for days, until I swept it off for the ants. Chub kept us company for three years and then one spring he just did not show up. We missed him. None of the other squirrels were as bold or friendly as good ol' Chub. I hope they have a place in Heaven for moochers. I'll gladly volunteer to be a moochee.

GOING TO THE DOGS

I've noticed that some folks like to get a dog or cat to keep them company in their senior years. I've had a dog most of my life, but Bob thinks that would be a foolish move to get one now because we travel so much. I hate to admit it, but he's right. Bob hasn't always been anti-dog, however. When Karen and David were little, he brought me a tiny Chihuahua home in his suit pocket. She was a cute little brown puppy and I named her Teena. Since I was in my knitting phase, I decided to knit her a sweater. She didn't really need a sweater, since we lived in California, but knitting kept me out of mischief. When I put it on her, she became top heavy and tipped over on her front legs. She couldn't even walk in her new sweater.

Queena, Bob's dog choice, was just the opposite. She was a tough, brawny Besenji, the breed that doesn't bark. But she could do everything else, including climbing trees and fences. She chewed up everything she could reach; the wires on our little lawn trailer, boards on our wooden gate, and limbs off our trees. She made her home in an old toy box with sliding doors, that we kept in the garage. One time when she got sick the vet gave us medicine that Bob had to shoot down her throat with a syringe. She didn't take well to the treatment and would hide down in the toy box where it was hard to reach her. So Bob slid the masonite doors closed assuming she could not get inside. He had no sooner gone back in the house when he heard, "Rrrippppp!" We ran back into the garage to see Queena ripping those doors right out of the box so she could get inside. She did get over the stomach aliment we were treating her for however. She'd swallowed the string off a roast she had found in our garbage and it had gummed up her insides.

On Pam's tenth birthday, we were shopping for her present when we saw a little beagle puppy in the pet store, begging for a home. I called Bob and asked if I could buy the puppy, and he answered with an emphatic, *"NO!"* We had moved into a new home, and were putting in the yard and didn't need a dog to help us dig.

Feeling a little rebellious, I bought the pup anyway, but let Pam carry it in the house to show her dad. He was *not* happy, and if it hadn't been for the kids, I think he would have put me up for adoption. However the pup, Abby, won all of our hearts except Bob's, and they had many running battles.

He loved to fish, but I hated to cook fish, and when our freezer got too full, I took the fish out and buried them in the garden for fertilizer. Bob came home from school and said, "Why are all my fish laying out on the back lawn?" Abby had dug them all up and laid them out on the grass. I was in big trouble again.

That Father's Day, Bob got a brand new pair of slippers. He said, "Do I need new slippers?"

"You do now," I confessed. "Abby chewed up your old pair." He learned to put his slippers up on the shelf when they were not on his feet. She didn't chew up anyone else's slippers, just Bob's.

We had a nice garden that year and Abby turned vegetarian. Bob had to battle her for the peas, tomatoes and carrots because she would grab them and run.

I thought Bob might like Abby better if she produced some income, so I decided to breed her to Taco, an AKC beagle down the street. She had four cute little pups, but she was a terrible mother. She refused to get into the box with them unless it was feeding time and when they got their teeth, she wouldn't get near them at all. Taco loved them. He'd come to our house and flip the mail slot on the door until we let him in. He would lay down in the box and let the pups crawl all over him. When it was time to feed the babies pablum, I had to shut Abby outside or she would eat the food before the pups could get enough. Even then she'd come in and lick it off their faces.

Abby loved the great out doors. A group of David's classmates went on a handcart trek and took Abby. She thought she'd gone to dog heaven. She had run and jumped and rolled and when she got home she smelled so bad that we had to give her a bath before we let her in the house.

She wasn't the smartest dog on the block though. David used to tell her to "stay" in the kitchen, while he hid on the stairs. We'd say, "Go find David," and she'd run out in the hall and look all around, but could never find him until he called to her. The sad part about it was that he hid in the same place every time. To help her, he even left a trail of popcorn, but she got so busy eating popcorn that she forgot what she was supposed to "find David."

In the past twenty years, we replaced dogs with horses for a time, but I still miss their furry little faces and slobbery kisses. In the future, however, when Bob dies I am going to buy a coffee table for the family room....and a dog. He says when I die he is going to sell our condo and move to California, without a dog.

MARCH OF THE ORANGE CONES

We moved to Draper in 2002, following a path of orange cones along the freeway clear from Highland. They weren't there to escort us to our new home, they were an indication of a work in progress. The state wanted a new improved freeway for the Winter Olympics crowd to admire when they arrived in Utah. It worked well, but since then, those cones have been *stalking* us.

After they finished I-15, the cones suddenly appeared on 114th South. Changes were coming. That street needed it too. It was so full of patches and giant potholes your hub caps could disappear and never be heard of again. When the orange cones come out, so do the humans with orange vests. The vest means you can move around the construction site freely, without actually doing any construction. The rules stipulate that when the vests work on the road, one guy does the work and three others lean on their shovels and watch. Well, 114th was torn up the better part of six months, but when it was finished it was a wonder to behold...all the way from State Street to 1300 East. But a mere week after the cones disappeared, they were back again. The road was not tilted enough for the water to run off to the side, and the whole thing had to be refinished at a new angle.

That lasted for one month, and then out came a few of the orange cones again, this time to mark the spot for the manhole covers to be placed in cement. Black top will not do for manholes...they have to be cement. For all intents and purposes the people at the sewer department, the communications department, and the street department, do not speak to each other. Each department does its own thing in its own due time.

We were safe from the orange cones for the winter, but in spring the ruling powers decided that State Street was in need of a fix, and out came the orange. Getting anywhere down town was an adventure in cone kill. When the freeway was blocked, cars got off onto State Street adding more congestion, and we just tried to stay out of the orange zone if we could. Our lives were defined by a sea of orange.

At the same time State street was full of cones, someone decided to repair 123rd South, complete with a new underpass at the State Street and I-15 intersection. That world of cones and confusion caused us to rear end a big truck. Nothing was hurt but our Highlander, our pride, and our good driver discount.

Now this spring, the orange cones are after us again. First they dug up our lovely 114th at 700 East. They dug a hole so big and deep that 14 Chinese guys climbed out and headed to medical school before they could put on the man hole cover. They dug up curbs, landscaping, and power poles. Traffic had to creep through the maze of cones and orange vested traffic controllers. They said this project will take a year to finish. In the meantime the orange cones have grown into tall orange barriers with orange flags flapping on top.

Take heed, fellow citizens! One morning you'll wake up and find guys with orange vests completely tearing up your street and surrounding it with orange cones, and you'll be forced to just sit in your house, read, and eat your food storage until a horse and buggy comes to rescue you.

Senior Living--
Day in, Day Out

When you're younger you can fly right over the bumps in the daily road. For seniors, the bumps require mountain climbing skills.

BATTLE OF THE BUGS

I'll tell you, there's a serious war going on, and I don't just mean the one in Iraq. I mean the war right here in Draper City, with a capital D that rhymes with B, and that stands for Bugs! It all started with our unusually cool, wet spring. I loved it, and so did my roses, and apparently, so did the bugs. When the weather started to warm up, those little buggers attacked in force.

The first wave was the tiny sugar ants. They weren't satisfied just to clean up in the garden. One morning we discovered an army of them had formed a solid line from the back door, along the edge of the tile, up the underside of the cupboard and onto the sink where they were carrying off some cookie crumbs. I tried to stem the tide with my bare toe, and the little scum bags bit me! I grabbed my insect spray and gunned them down, and won the skirmish...temporarily.

Then came the fruit flies. Although they are slow, it was hard to take a deep breath without inhaling the darn pests. Our grandson went on the computer and found out how to make a trap by putting a rotten banana in a bottle, covering the top with shrink wrap, and making some tiny pinholes. The flies go inside, but lack the smarts to get out again. This seemed to work, but I thought if the pinholes were bigger, more flies could get in. NOT! I created a fly brothel and they crawled in, found a mate, and whole families of them crawled back out into the house to fly around and annoy us. So I made another bottle with tiny holes and this worked for all but one or two flies, and those we whacked with high technology; a rolled up newspaper.

Next invasion came from aphids, who were bent on shredding my beautiful roses. So, armed with my trusty insect spray gun, I set up a new battle front on my patio. I fought valiantly until driven indoors by a deadly swarm of mosquitoes who were trying to drink my type A blood and give me the West Nile Virus.

The latest invasion to our city are the dreaded grasshoppers. They are not as thick here in the city as they are out in the country where they cover the fields and houses. The farm folk have to crunch their way up their driveways and sweep them off their front doors. Where are the seagulls when you need them? Oh, wait. The seagulls did come and ate as many as their little tummies would hold, like in a scene straight from the *Brigham Young* movie. I tried to hire a squadron of gulls to fly over my house twice a day on a hunt and kill mission, but I don't speak twitter.

These six-legged pests eat our clothes, our food, our houses, and even us, but I think I have a way to win this war. Let's turn the tables and learn to eat the bugs. I have tasted chocolate covered grasshoppers and fried silk worms. The grasshoppers weren't too bad, but the silk worms were horrible and when I spit them out, my saliva had turned green. We could try to add some chocolate covered ants to our cookie dough. We could make Shoo Fly Pie with real flies, and a nice pot of mosquito stew would be zesty. So we can wage cruel war on the bugs and perhaps they'll erect a bronze statue of us by the seagull monument on Temple Square, with a cooking pot in our hand.

JEANNIE'S BEANIES

You hear a lot about multi-tasking these days, but I've been doing it for years. In high school I always loved to listen to the radio while I did my homework, which accounted for my less-than-perfect grades, I'm sure. Now days when I sit down to watch some mindless TV show, I usually draw, solve Sudoku puzzles, or crochet.   Lately I've become obsessed with crocheting cute little cloche type hats that resemble helmets with a big crochet flower on the side. My friend gave me a pattern, and with some left over gold yarn I was able to whip one up while spending the evening with *Dancing With The Stars*, without even dropping a stitch. I put an orange, pink, and red flower on the gold hat, so my next project was to use up the rest of the orange multicolor yarn in a hat with a gold flower. Then came the Big Encouragement. Grand daughter Katie's friends came over to visit and saw the hat collection. They "Oooo'd" and "Aaaa'd" and pronounced them "awesome!" I was so encouraged that I marched right out and bought fuzzy pink yarn, purple variegated yarn, turquoise yarn, and red, white and blue yarn. I was in business, crocheting to my little heart's content.

Before long, Bob began to notice all the hats laid out on the back of the couch and asked me to declare my intentions. Well, I really hadn't intended to keep them all. I have enough collections already, so when my sister-in-law Carol came over and requested one to give her ailing sister, I gave her two. Taryn and Andrea came home from SUU for the weekend and I managed to hide a gold hat and a blue multicolored hat in their luggage before they went back. Katie's friends came over and took a couple more home, and I found my supply dwindling down. The red, white and blue hats were the only ones not finding a home, but then who wants to wear a hot hat in July?

Grandson Kurt and his wife Kelsey have a beautiful baby girl, Alexandra Jane, whose tiny little head needed a pink hat, and I was crocheting again. The hat was a little big, but should be just right for an Easter bonnet in April when they bless her. Kurt, a student at UVU has always had a flair for the unusual, and even went to high school on Halloween dressed as Cupid in pink tights. He liked my hats, but the flower was too much. He requested bear ears on his black hat instead. Well guess what...two large flower pedals make great ears, and Kurt has his bear hat to wear to work while he makes pizzas to support his family and his education. I didn't leave Kelsey out, either. She has a pink fuzzy hat with ears and Ally Jane had to have a pink hat with ears to match her parents. It's a family thing.

Now I'm working on my latest masterpiece...a red, black, and yellow hat with dreadlocks and multicolored beads hanging down. Folks will ask, "Did Jamaica hat, mon?" And I'll say, "Ya mon, wid me lil crochet hook!" I think it may go to high school with David on Hat Day. It's just the thing for a high school English teacher to wear.

Oh, wait. Does all this crocheting make me the family hooker?

SUPER GAME DAY

I've been so excited lately to read that some cities were urging families to get together once a week for a game day. I was also happy to see all the snacks being offered by local markets for a family game day. Families should do stuff together.

"Bob," sez I, "Shall I buy a selection of those snacks and we can have a game day too?" I pulled out my Catch Phrase game, and I was ready to defeat all challengers.

Bob shook his head at me and said, "Look Babe. The whole world is having a game day this Sunday afternoon. It's called *Super Bowl XLIV*."

"Oh, yeah...right," I said, as I hid my Catch Phrase game between the couch cushions. I know about the Super Bowl. They made a movie about one a few years ago where bad guys were planning to blow it up, but I have never watched a game from beginning to end. In past years I have used a TV that had picture in picture and watched a DVD with the Super Bowl in the corner. Then when I saw yelling from the football fans, I switched the PIP to see what they were excited about. I began to think I was missing something wonderful, so I decided this was the year for me to really see the Super Bowl.

First, I had to know who was playing. It's required that you have to develop feelings for one team or the other. There were the Saints from New Orleans, and the Colts from somewhere in Indiana. I did a lot of scientific research and studied the stats, and chose to cheer for the Colts because they had pretty blue uniforms and Austin Colley from BYU.

Since Bob and I are trying to lose weight, I cut out all the pictures of high calorie snacks, and taped them on the cupboard by our rice cakes and diet sodas, so we could see all the calories we were missing. We turned on the fireplace and the TV, and I was good to go!

The first half was wonderful, and I got carried away, yelling and waving my arms around. After the first Colt's touchdown, Bob took his snacks and moved to the other side of the room. He claimed I kept smacking him on the arm, and he didn't want bruises.

Then came the half time. I'm just not young enough to understand The Who (or Whatever) and guys yelling at the top of their lungs, trying to force loud music through my head. That is not my idea of fun. So I pushed the mute button and went into the kitchen to make a sandwich. And who should I find, but Bob, loading up on milk and double-stuffed Oreos. He'd had enough diet foods snacks for the day.

During the second half of the game I was more subdued, and by the end I was right down disappointed. However, I did shed a sentimental tear when quarterback Breez held up his little boy to share in the excitement of the crowd. I do hope the kid gets to go to Disney World with the team.

There is still a lot about football I don't understand. What's the difference between a referee and an umpire? Why did the Colt quarterback sit with his cap on, staring into space during the second half? And why do they put up a net to catch the football when it's kicked? It seems to me they could let the crowd have a chance at it.

The Olympics are coming next and I'm already in training with my blanket, my recliner, and my hot chocolate, low fat of course.

SHOE FETISH

Yes...I'll admit that I have a shoe fetish. That's me, who likes to run around in my bare naked feet 24-6, because on the seventh day the Lord saith, "Thou must wear shoes to church." So sez I, "Why not wear the best looking shoes you can on that day?" My mom fed my fetish by saving my baby shoes, that are now bronzed bookends. During WW II when you had to have a ration coupon to buy a pair of shoes, my dad donated all of his coupons to me, because my feet were still growing, and he made do with half soles on the same pair of shoes for four years.

When I hit middle school, (or junior high, as we called it) I needed *Joyce* shoes to go with my *Jantzen* sweaters and matching socks. The shoes were expensive at $9 a pair, and I contracted with my dad to mow the lawn twice a week, all summer long, with an old ornery push mower, for a pair of navy blue suede *Joyces* for my feet and a red *Jantzen* for my top. I stitched up a navy blue wool skirt to complete the ensemble and I was hot stuff!

My first year in high school saddle shoes were all the rage. My saddle shoes had to be polished with a liquid that resembled buttermilk, so every night I borrowed one of my mother's water color brushes to meticulously apply the polish around the saddle part of the shoe. She complained that shoe polish ruined her brush, and was glad when saddle shoes were out of style.

The saddles shoes gave way to white buck shoes which were much easier to keep clean. All you had to do was brush up the nap, smack them with a bag of powdered chalk substance once a day and you were stylin'.

Bob came home from Korea in 1952, and brought some unique foot wear that fit between the toes. They were called Jap flaps. As we became friendly with the Japanese, we substituted the more politically correct name, zories. They became so popular that everyone had a pair or two and we just called them thongs. Now when I ask my grandkids how I look in my new thongs, they fall on the floor laughing, imagining me wearing some racy underwear. The shoes are now called flip-flops. I wonder what's next...just flops?

The highlight of my shoe collecting however, was when we were living in Southern Cal, and a store named Bakers had a sale on their sample shoes twice a year. Sample shoes were size 4 ½ B and they cost $1.49, and that was for both shoes! I was sure I had died and gone to shoe heaven. I could actually afford three or four pair at a time. The day the sale began, I'd run the kids up to visit my mom, and off I'd go. It got to be quite a joke. Bob would go into the closet, drag all my shoes into the living room and ask, "Do you really need more shoes," like *need* has anything to do with it. When we moved back to Utah, it took three big boxes just to haul my shoes. My daughters and all their friends loved my shoes until they got to be teenagers and their feet got too big to fit into them.

I still have lots of shoes; six pair of flops, satin slippers with marabou feathers, gold, beaded silver, clear, water shoes, winter boots, cowboy boots, etc. My latest acquisitions came from an Easy Spirit store that went out of business. I love their comfortable shoes, so I bought several pairs at $9.00 a pop. My favorites were brown sling pumps, with sharp pointy toes and big brass buckles. First time I got them out to wear, I noticed something amiss. Both shoes were for the right foot. Bob said, "Didn't you try both of them on?" I didn't have time. I was trying to grab my share of shoes before someone else discovered the sale.

The store is now empty and locked up, so I guess if I wear my new shoes, it will be the two right ones. If you see me limping, I'll lie to you and say my knees are hurting. I can't let a brand new pair of shoes go to waste now, can I?

JEANNIE APPLESEED

Bob and I get to volunteer at the LDS Church's Welfare Square and this particular time they were bottling applesauce. I'd like to be noble and claim that we did it because of President Obama's call for all Americans to put forth a day of service to others, but it is really because the membership of our church ward consists of the newly weds and the nearly deads, and we couldn't get anyone else to volunteer. So six a.m. rolled around, and I dragged my pitiful self from under the warm blankets, combed my hair, plastered down the wrinkles on my face and off we went to do a service.

When we arrived, they presented us with the latest fashion in lovely hairnets, plastic aprons and gloves, and took us to the line where the clean apples came down the chute onto a conveyor belt. Our job was to place the apple, stem side up into a cup that swung it inside a giant noisy machine with whirling blades. The blades cut the core out of the apple. We were warned not to put our hands any closer to the blades than the outer edge of the cup, and to illustrate, there were graphic drawings at eye level, of a hand with fingers cut off and red blood dripping out. It scared the bejebbers out of me, as I like my hands just the way they are, arthritis and all.

I was stationed at the first of the line where the buttons were located that said START, STOP, and OOPS. After the explanation, the nice man in charge pushed the start button, a horn blared and everything began to move. All went well, until I noticed that some of the leaves and large stems were still connected to the apples. So I appointed myself quality control officer, and began pulling out the twigs, leaves, mashed apples, and even the occasional cell phone. Wait just a minute...a cell phone? Yes, somehow a cell phone had made it down the line, through the wash and onto the conveyor belt. Bob rescued it and took it back to the washing room, but no one there claimed it. Who knows how long the poor little phone had been in the company of bad apples, but it had really been beat up. As quality control officer, I pronounced it dead, and took it to the lost and found office.

The apple line seemed to be going well, although I was not as good at getting the apples exactly centered as possible. I sure was not going to reach into that machine once it started to swing the apple into the cutting blades. Besides, I was busy with my quality control work. And then something went terribly wrong. In pulling a tough bundle of leaves off the top of an apple, my elbow whipped back and pushed the OOPS button. An alarm screamed and the conveyor belts and the machines all stopped. The supervisor rushed over and yelled, "What happened?" All of the other workers pointed at me and slowly backed away leaving me standing there with my bare face hanging out.

"Sorry," I stammered. "I washed my elbows, and I can't do a thing with them." He glared at me. Then he stripped away my plastic apron, my plastic gloves, and my hairnet, and chucked them in the trash, and marched me out to sit in the lost and found office with the dead cell phone until Bob came to claim me at the end of the shift.

The ride home was very quiet. Bob mumbled something about not taking me around machinery ever again, but I'm sure he'll forget and change his mind in a year or two!

HIGH SCHOOL REUNION - 60th ?!

Well, I dragged Bob kicking and protesting to his 60th Provo
High School reunion. Since he left Provo after graduating from
BYU, he didn't feel that he'd know, or even care about a bunch of
old duffers, especially since they were charging $75 a couple.
Who can eat $75 worth of food no matter how good it tastes?
But we put on our happy faces and drove down to the Marriott
Hotel in Provo and made our grand entrance. Bob looked all
around the room and recognized Mel (or Del) Taylor, a twin who
seems to turn up at all reunions, including my BY High School
gatherings every year that we've had one. Good, we knew at
least one person.

The display at the door was a Wall of Remembrance with
pictures of all the dead folks, which seemed to included about a
third of the class. We did know several of them. They pinned a
badge on Bob with his name and high school picture. I must
admit that Bob is one who has grown more handsome as a senior
citizen, but then I'm a little prejudiced. We wandered around
looking like lost souls until one lady came up to Bob, looked at his
name tag, then his face and admitted, "Bob Moore? I don't
remember you at all."

"That's understandable," sez he. "I was in the Witness
Protection Program in high school and used a different name."

"Oh what name was that?" she inquired innocently?

"Well, I could tell you, but then I have to kill you," he said,
without even cracking a smile. She backed slowly away and stood
against the Wall of Remembrance. I pulled him over to a chair at
the dark end of the room, and we sat down with three other

couples who were strangers to us. Where's Mel when you need him?

As we sat down, a sweet old lady behind me said, "Aren't you Jean Anderson?"

"I was," I confessed, "but I've been Jean Moore for 55 years now."

"Do you remember me? I went to BY High with you, and my name was Mary Louise Clark."

Did I remember her? I'll be indebted to her forever and ever. She gave Bob my telephone number in high school and told him we were just right for each other. He called me and made a date and the rest is history! I squealed like a high school girl and gave her a big hug. Finally, I had someone to talk to. I didn't make it to my last reunion but Mary Louise filled me in on those still among the living. She said one of our classmates sat down by her and said, "Now don't take this the wrong way, but of all the people here, I think you are the one who's changed the most. You look so different, Sybil."

She answered, "Maybe that's because I'm not Sybil Clark...I'm Mary Louise Clark." We both had a good laugh.

At the end of a very interesting slide show, door prizes were handed out. I got hot pads, and Bob got a nice boxed pen. Then they asked all the people who had pens to stand up. "You five are the committee for the next reunion!" In disgust, Bob threw his pen down on the floor, but I made him go pick it up and play nice. The evening ended with an argument over whether to meet again in two years or five. One old lady said, " Too many of us will be dead in five years. Let's meet again in two years."

Bob *kindly* pointed out that the same people would be dead in five years whether they had a two year reunion or not. He suggested that those who had passed on could have their own ghostly reunion. I don't think he'll be invited to any more reunions, and I don't think he cares.

PINCHING THE LINCOLNS

Bob admits to being Danish with a little Irish thrown in, but hotly denies there is any Scottish in his ancestry. His actions prove otherwise, however. That man can squeeze a penny so hard that tears come to Lincoln's eyes. And this is a good thing for our family because the dollars seem to fly right through my fingers, and Bob's penny pinching has kept us solvent during our 56 years of marriage.

When we were in grade school you could get into the movies with 14 cents and the cap off of a bottle of milk. When he took a date to the movie, he had a bottle cap for her, but she had to furnish her own 14 cents. Knowing Bob, I think she may have had to buy her own popcorn too.

After we were married and both students at BYU, Bob would go deer hunting in the fall and we would eat venison roasts, steaks, chops, and even ground venison all year. That was our meat supply and I learned to really hate venison.

We were able to have cheap date nights in college thanks to brother Stan and Carol. Every Sunday night we would drive out to their little house in Orem, watch Ed Sullivan on TV, and eat chocolate malt cake. We had no TV, and just a few cake crumbs at our own tiny apartment.

When we got out of school, tile work was stylish but very expensive, so Bob learned how to tile and grout. He made a kitchen table, a coffee table and a pair of lamps for the living room.

He wanted to learn to sew. He never used a pattern but he improvised well. When Karen needed a dress for YWCA Indian

Maidens, he had her lay down on a piece of brown material with her neck at the fold, and then traced around her with piece of chalk. He sewed all the seams and put some nice fringe on the sleeves. Then I did the tracing and he sewed a matching shirt for himself.

He and David joined Indian Guides and Bob out did himself. He bought yellow caps, and bags and bags of yellow pin feathers. He put beaks and eyes on the caps, and covered them with small feathers, and then cut large yellow wings out of felt. He attached each pin feather to the wings individually. It took him many weeks, but he and David were the hit of all the city parades that summer performing the Soaring Eagle dance in their handmade yellow chicken suits, that put most Indians to shame.

Bob was especially thrifty when it came to greeting cards. While we were in college, he'd take me to the Hallmark store and I'd pick out the card I liked, read it and put it back on the rack. After we had graduated and were earning a little money, he was more bold. I picked out my anniversary and my birthday card, and he actually bought them. That was nice, except he kept giving me the same cards year after year until I tired of them and secretly threw them away.

We buy cars that are several years old, and Bob's fame for bargaining with used car dealers is legendary. He once told a car salesman who was following us around talking, "If bull crap were music, you'd be a whole brass band!" I don't think the salesman understood what that meant because he just kept following us with a big grin on his face. Nowadays when our grandkids are looking for cars, they come to their grandpa to ask for advice, or to do the haggling for them.

Bob likes to donate blood. I do not, as I need every drop I have in my little body. But he always hangs a guilt trip on me by telling me my blood would be saving some little child's life, and besides, if I'd donate blood he'd take me to lunch. Ever a sucker for eating out, I'd go donate my precious pint and then he'd take me next door to the R. C. Willey Furniture Store where they serve free hot dogs and Cokes on the weekends.

Yesterday I saw him cut an article out of the paper that shows how to build your own coffin. You build it, put shelves in it, and use it for a curio cabinet prior to its final use. You don't suppose he's so tight he'd do something like that do you?

COLOR MY WORLD

Who would ever guess that a drawing of John Wayne would lead me into #7 on my bucket list? There I was, walking through the craft store, and his smoldering eyes were inviting me to come take a colored pencil class to draw him, then hang him in my home. I thought colored pencils belonged in the kid's department. Was I ever wrong!

So I paid my money and joined up. There was just one other lady, me and a teacher named Bunny. She did not let me start on the Duke, however. First I had to draw spheres, shaded squares, and pegs with graphite. Next I had to draw an eye. The other lady was creating beautiful roses in vibrant colors. When could I work with color?

That was lesson four and Bunny brought me a lion cub on the rocks to draw...not the real thing. Just a picture. Well I was hooked. I loved the color and the class. Colored pencil work is slow and labor intensive, but produces some wonderful results and it doesn't stink like oil paints. Our class grew and we kept busy making the world a more colorful place.   One member of our original class began doing portraits on commission and now teaches classes of her own. She still drops in from time to time to visit and get inspiration from her old buddies.

People would come and go, including Bunny who moved to Mesquite, but Kathi took her place and now there are eight of us who have been together for over seven years. I'm the oldest person at 76 and the youngest is an exuberant 45. Although we are all women, we've come from many different backgrounds, including one lady whose mother was a snake charmer. We, *The Pencil Pushers*, are more than an art group. We review books and movies and share the ones we consider worthy. We give advice freely and accept criticism. We sometimes burst out in spontaneous singing. We laugh together and even cry together. Most of all, we enjoy each other's company.

I'm not going to name all the ladies, because my cast of characters in this book is already very large, but we do have some funny things happen with our art projects from time to time.

One of our members was drawing an apparently cursed picture. It was a landscape with an old cabin under a beautiful rainbow. She had finished the sky and the rainbow, when a little piece of the paper fell out leaving a small hole in her work. Not to be discouraged, she started over on a new piece of paper. She was sitting by a river while her husband fished, when a dog climbed up the bank and shook himself, making spots all over the second attempt. We assured her the third time would be the charm. This time she left her work safely in the back seat of the car. Her husband tossed an empty pop can into the back, and there was just enough liquid to spot the bottom of the picture. Kathi thinks she can draw a river over the spots, even though rivers usually don't bubble.

I found a picture of Christ I liked. He is holding on to the spar of a boat and he is laughing. I worked so hard on that picture to get everything right. When it was finished, I brought it home to show Bob and Katie. They took one look and said, "Nice picture of Kenny Loggins." Loggins?! That was supposed to be Jesus. Silly family!

All of us have drawn portraits of some kind. At times they turn out well, and at other times we start over. One of our group was drawing a picture of her father-in-law, when Kathi came over to check. "What are you drawing by the side of his head," she asked?

"That's the lamp on the table behind him," was the explanation.

"When you're doing a portrait, you don't have to draw every thing you see. Keep it simple." She told us about her first drawing of a child leaning against a pillow and she even drew the *Do not remove* tag on the pillow.

Colored pencils are expensive so we try to use them right down to the nub. We tape the old pencil to the top of a new one and use it until we can no longer get it into the pencil sharpener. I've been gathering up all the little nubs with the hope of getting someone to make a nice necklace for me. It occurs to me that I've been living with Bob so long, I can pinch a penny just as hard as he can.

TWILIGHT ZONED

I can fly on a kestrel. I can push a handcart. I can love a vampire, and all within the walls of my own home. One advantage of being a senior citizen is having time to read the books on your bucket list. That day has come!

I remember reading my first storybook in kindergarten class for sharing time. I knew all the words but *island.* I was devastated that the teacher had to correct my pronunciation of "is-land."

That didn't dampen my love affair with books, however. In grade school I read every *Oz* book in the library. When I wanted to read *Moby Dick,* the librarian told me I would have to go upstairs to the adult library, but I wasn't old enough to get a card there yet. Once I started a book, it was hard for me to put it down. It was like being in the twilight zone and I was no longer in control. I would sneak a flashlight into my bedroom at night and read under the covers until my mother caught me, and confiscated my flashlight. What a bummer!

In college I met the classics, and I was drawn to historical heroines like *Jane Eyre* and *Little Women*. I loved Charles Dickens' books too, although the formal language made them slow reading. I still read *A Christmas Carol* every year, and laugh with delight when Scrooge discovers it's Christmas Day and he's not too late to work some magic of his own.

As a teacher, I scheduled story time after lunch each day. I could really ham it up with Dr. Seuss, *Winnie the Pooh* and *Charlotte's Web.* I always cried when the spider died at the end. Who cries over a stupid spider?

Bob caught me sitting on a pile of clean laundry one day, zoned out in the *Twilight* book. "Why don't you finish this work?" he said, breaking into my reverie.

"This is my work.. I am helping Edward and Bella fight the Volturi."

"Yeah...right," he scoffed.

On any given day, if you come to visit our condo you will find Bob and I with our noses in books. Bob's taste in literature is different from mine. He likes westerns with a little John Grisham thrown in for flavor. I like to curl up in my chair at night with Stephenie Meyers, J. K. Rowling, and Suzanne Collins. I know...they are young adult books, but I am young at heart.

Stephenie Meyer's *Twilight* series have turned me into a "Twihard." I have read the series of books more times than I care to admit. Each time a new *Twilight* movie comes out I'm obligated to reread the books and watch the three DVD's I now own. Therefore, I have established a Halloween tradition. I take my *Twilight* books and DVD's into my family room with the big screen TV, and spend the night with the vampires, red velvet chocolate cake, and a big glass of milk with ice in it. You're welcome to come over to my twilight zone but you have to bring your own snacks, because I have trouble sharing my cake.

I'm not quite so obsessive with the *Harry Potter* series. They are exciting, but there are so many Potter books and DVD's now, that it would take several weeks to reread every one when a new movie comes out. I do enjoy watching the DVD's when Katie lets me borrow them, but they take two or three days to finish, and she doesn't like them out of her possession that long. Rotten grandkids!

I enjoyed Suzanne Collins' series, *The Hunger Games.* Sometimes her characters don't have the moral fortitude of Edward the vampire or Harry the wizard who both try to do what's right with the world. Katness is courageous but fails to give Peeta credit for all he does for her.

For Christmas I'm hoping Santa will bring me one of those new Nook readers. Can you imagine having an entire library in one little skinny computer? I can carry it with me 24/7 and zone out as long as my eyes last. Wonderful!

THANKS FOR THE MEMORIES...WHEREVER THEY ARE

One of the problems we encounter as seniors is a loss of memory. I don't mean the real serious kinds like dementia or Alzheimer, but the silly ones like, what did I have for breakfast this morning? It's like we're studying for the *hereafter* when we die. We walk into the kitchen, stand there with a lost look on our face and say, "What in the heck am I *hereafter*?" Be patient, however. You'll remember as soon as you walk back out of the kitchen.

I'm convinced that there is a little gatekeeper that runs around in the folds of our brain, trying his best to plug into the answers we are seeking. But he is getting older too, and has to sit down and rest occasionally. That is why the information comes to us more slowly now.

Take heart, ladies. In a new Mayo clinic study of men and women over 70, they found that men were almost 50% more likely to suffer from mild cognitive impairment, including memory lapses. So if your man forgets your birthday and anniversary, he now has an excuse...he's old! But you can add some gentle reminders. Paint "It's my birthday today," across your forehead with magic markers. Stand right under his nose until he reads it. Or you can always buy yourself that strand of pearls you're wanted and put the gift box by your plate at dinner. Then you tell him, "Thank you for the lovely birthday gift!" He'll congratulate himself for remembering.

Bob and I give ourselves many memory helps. We have a small calendar book and we try to write all of our appointments, special days, when to pay bills, etc. in that book. When we can remember where that book is...we check it from time to time to find out what we've missed.

There is always the old tying a string around the finger memory trick. It works well if you can recall where you keep the string. I try turning the ring on my hand backwards. That becomes very annoying as I try to grip things, and I unconsciously turn it back around and forget everything.

Car keys are a constant problem, so Bob hung a key holder by the back door. Along comes some security know-it-all who says, "Don't hang keys by the back door. Put them by your bed and if someone tries to break into your home, press the panic button and your car will start to beep. That will scare the bad guys away." And also scares the heck out of the neighbors. Now if we can just decide whose side of the bed gets the keys. Is it Bob, who can't hear anything, or me who hears every little noise because I can't sleep?

For years I have had trouble keeping track of my purse. As we leave the house every day, I grab my purse. Bob sez, "Why are you taking your purse? Are you planning to buy something?" Obviously men do not understand the enormity of the secret things in a woman's purse. Besides money, there's makeup, *Reader's Digest*, aspirin, tissues, band aids, hand cleaner, flashlight, measuring tape, snack bars, cell phone, and a compass. Who knows when I'm going to be called upon to save the world with the contents from my purse? But as important to me as it is, I have left it sitting in restaurants more times than I care to admit. The latest was just a month ago, and as we pulled into the garage at home I reached down for my purse and there was nothing but air. Bob is never happy when we have to go back to retrieve my precious purse, but he doesn't say anything. My mind is racing through all the credit cards, driver's license, and things I must cancel immediately. I must have a great guardian angel though, because my purse has always been saved by some honest person and everything is intact.

Names are another thing easy to forget, and that's not just new names. I sometimes forget my family names. At Christmas when all the grand kids are around, my gatekeeper blacks out. So I communicate by pointing and saying, "You girl," or "You boy," until the person I want is standing in front of me saying, "What, Gram?"

By then I've forgotten what I wanted, so I look them right in the eye and say, "What are you *hereafter,* anyway?"

Living with Non-Senior Families

We make adjustments in our senior years. We can't remember why. We just do.

MIGHTY MOM

My mom was just a little lady all of 5'2" high, but she had a large heart. This was both a physical ailment (an enlarged heart due to childhood disease) and a heart full of love for her bumbling little girl, and I gave her heart plenty of exercise. Thanks to me, Mom became a world class worrier. Take the incident of the baby ducks for example. I was five when I came home from the carnival with a small box of quackers. My friend Earle had won two little yellow baby ducks and had given them to me, as he didn't dare take them home himself. My mom allowed me to keep the ducks, if I would take care of them. So I promised her, with all my childish fervor, that I would tend them forever. My dad got a sturdy wooden Hercules Powder box, and we put in some water and mash, and strips of rags hanging down in one corner to keep my ducks warm. Several times during the day, the ducks and I strolled around the yard, with me as the leader, and the ducks waddling along behind. One day Mom decided the little fellars needed a swim, so she filled a tub with water, and because there was no way for them to get in or out by themselves, my job was to watch and take them out when they got tired. All went well for a while, but my attention span was short, and who knew ducks could get water logged? Next thing I knew, my worried momma was yelling at me, as she pulled two little dripping bodies from the bottom of the tub. I started to cry. I had let my ducks down, literally. Mighty Mom ran into the house and got some whiskey in an eye dropper. She took each of the little ducks, pumped its wings back and forth to get the water out, and then gave it a shot of booze. The ducks commenced quacking and running around in crazy circles, and then settled down in a patch of sunlight until their down dried out. Mom didn't say much, but I could tell she was disappointed in my birding skills.

A few weeks later, dad built a nice pen outside for my ducks, and when they grew too big for that, we took them out to a farm where there were other ducks and a big pond. My ducks never even looked back to say goodbye, the ingrates, and they lived happily ever after with their new ducky friends.

I've never felt life was a spectator sport, and in kindergarten I wanted to participate in Show and Tell every day. I raised my hand as I thought, "What am I going to say?" Then I remembered my birthday was coming up, so I invited the whole class to my birthday party. What a great idea! I happened to have a very wise teacher, and she called my mom to tell her what had happened. I'm sure my worried mom's heart skipped a beat as she envisioned 32 six-year-olds running through our little house. She and the teacher decided that bringing cupcakes to all the kids at school would fill the obligation and keep me from being disgraced. So Mighty Mom and her cupcakes saved the day again.

We didn't take a lot of vacations, so when we did it was cause for great anxiety. Mom always insisted that we carry snacks, sleeping bags, and prune juice in the trunk of the car. When we went to Mexico, we even included a tent with our luggage. We drove across the border at Mexicali, and went down to Guaymas. Mom took one look at the local motels and insisted Dad get reservations at the fancy American hotel up on the hill. It was very nice, although it must have been pricey, but Dad thought it was worth it so that mom wouldn't worry about being murdered in her sleep.

She worried about me until I got married, and then she worried about my children. When Karen was born, she came to stay with us, and every time Bob tried to take a picture, Mom put her hand over the baby's face so the light wouldn't hurt her eyes. As result, we don't have any pictures of Karen's face until she was over a month old.

Mom passed on many years ago, but she is probably waiting by the Golden Gate, worried about whether I'll be able to get in or not.

DAD WAS ELECTRIFYING

I don't know exactly when my dad fell in love with electricity, because as a boy there were very few homes that even had that power. My dad, Theo, was the oldest in a family of six boys and one girl, growing up in rural Idaho, but he found a small hand-cranked generator in a catalog and saved enough money to buy it. He connected it to his mother's clothes line that consisted of two wooden poles with cross beams on top and four wires stretching from pole to pole. Dad connected his generator to the wires of the clothes line, and told his brothers to hold on. Then he gave the generator a crank, and his brothers got a nice zap! Boys, being what they are, thought that was great fun, and soon all the neighborhood kids were paying a penny to get zapped on the Anderson's clothes line.

When the family moved to Heber, Utah they had a farm house that was modern to the degree that there was one electric light bulb hanging from the ceiling in the kitchen. Papa Anderson, thinking electricity had medicinal purposes, used to unscrew the bulb and stick his finger in the socket. It gave him a little jolt that he said made his rheumatism better.

Dad was small in height at 5'6", but he was big on intelligence, and he graduated from the University of Utah with a degree in electrical engineering. That qualified him to do all sorts of fun stuff.

In 1946, Dad built the first electric lawn mower in Provo. He mounted a grinding wheel motor on the side of a old push mower, and connected a belt from the motor to the wheels of the mower. It then became my job to mow the lawn with his invention, and it worked great except for the few times I accidentally ran over and cut the cord.

One year for Halloween Dad made a special witch hat for Mom. He wired the brim with bubble lights, and on the top of the cone he rigged a bright red blinker light. It was all run with batteries in a flashlight hidden on the inside of the hat, so it could be turned on and off. He gave the hat to Mom, who added spiders and spider webs. It was an stunning creation.

A friend of the family, John, was going to celebrate his 40th birthday. John's wife, Alice, came to Dad and asked if he could design something memorable for the big party. So Dad went over to their house and carefully wove tiny copper wires through the upholstered seat of a dining room chair. To finish off his work, he hid a battery with a button in back of the chair that when pushed sent a small electrical current through the wires. There was a party of 30 unsuspecting people in attendance, and the scene was set. John sat in the chair while they sang the birthday song. Dad was at the other end of the room, and Alice stood behind the chair. As the song came to an end, Alice pushed the button. John rose up out of the chair like a rocket, and yelled, "Theo Anderson...I'll get you for this!" The room must have been filled with a bunch of masochists because many of them wanted to try the electric chair. I even tried it...once and once only.

After running electrical power plants in Nevada and Utah, Dad and Mom moved to California in 1957, and Dad helped design the guidance system for the Minute Man Missile, a more serious application of his talent.

Christmas was the time for my electrical dad to shine, and he pulled out all the stops in decorating their hillside home in 1965. There were lights all over the roof. There were spotlights on a custom painted Santa, sleigh, and reindeer, and assorted little animals by the front door. But the highlight was the beautiful aluminum tree inside their living room picture window. It had a changing color wheel, and the tree itself was mounted on a turn table, so it was slowly spinning also. This dazzling electrical display earned Dad first prize in the home decorating contest that year.

Dad has been gone for many years now, but I think that by the time I get to the pearly gates, he will have them electrified so I can just push a button and sneak right through before the angels realize I've died .

LIVE NATIVITY ADVENTURE

One of the adventures that Bob and I have every year is to be part of the live Nativity that our church presents in December. They have been doing this for fourteen years now, and without any outside advertising, hundreds and hundreds of people attend. They come from as far south as Nevada and as far north as Idaho, and they stand in line in the cold for hours waiting their turn to enter the city of Bethlehem.

The whole process starts right after Halloween, our way of chasing off the evil spirits. A huge semi pulls a trailer up to the pavilion in back of the stake center where awaits about fifty men and women and various scout troops, anxious to begin the creative work of building Bethlehem. Armed with hammers and hatchets, the boys want to build something right now, and I think many nails are driven into the black top and the dead grass before things get organized. After they off load the wooden walls and outdoor scenery, there are eighty carefully marked plastic bags holding costumes for the actors.

The men begin by laying out a path of straw and sawdust. Then they build walls and shops for the merchants with woven curtained entries. The last section is the manger, with room for Mary and Joseph to display their newborn babe to the folk of the village. This is all built under the protective roof of the pavilion at the end of the walk. They add lighting and a sound system to the outside and inside, with special attention to a warming light above the manger to keep Baby Jesus comfortable so "no crying he makes." There are actually four or five babies with their parents, so they can change cast members in the manger every hour if needed.

Besides the live cast members, it's the extra things that make this Bethlehem special. Many bales of hay are brought in and placed in strategic locations on the path. Palm fronds are hauled up from St. George and nailed to the top of poles for trees. Food for the animals is distributed in specific locations around the set, and there is wood chopped to feed the fires in the eight large braziers set around the parking lot to keep people warm on their trip to Bethlehem.

But one of the best features of the nativity is all the live animals that are brought into town. There are always camels, sheep, and goats. There is a patient little donkey that has stood by the manger every year of the show. The chickens this year were especially cooperative. They tended to hang out at the manger, because it is warm and a great places to roost. But when they got too numerous, we would just pick them up and haul them to another site. This event is one that Bob and I love, so we are there from the first day to the last. We spend one night as "exit greeters" and get to wear costumes from head to toe over our winter coats and boots. I found that holding a chicken kept me warmer, so I packed a one around with me for four hours.

The reenactment goes from six to nine p.m. but if there are people still in line, we just keep going until everyone gets a chance to see the Christ Child. This project lasts for four nights with a different cast each time, and then everything is taken down and packed away in the trailer for another year.

Now travel with me back to Bethlehem. It's dark as you journey down the path. You pass a pavilion where a prophet of God is reading scrolls that foretell of the birth of the savior. Further on, you pass the pavilion of the wise men as they are preparing their gifts for the journey. Their live camels stand by their side ready to go.

Wandering through the streets are peddlers and children, selling straw, gourds, and bread. Here comes a man with his herd of real goats.

As the path reaches Bethlehem you pass the money changer in his booth counting money. If you watch closely you may catch him sneaking a coin into his own pocket. There is a curtain at the entrance to the city where a Roman soldier stands guard and bids you enter the town.

It is much warmer inside and as the path curves around, there are shops with weavers, carpenters, and bakers. There are women drawing water, and even lepers in one dark corner ringing bells to warn people of their disease.

As you come up to the last corner, the inn keeper steps out of the doorway and tells you "no room in the inn." As you round the corner there it is...the manger, with Baby Jesus and his parents, basking in a beautiful warm light and looking absolutely heavenly. You are allowed to stay at the manger as long as you wish and as you leave you may have to wipe away a tear or two. It seems so real.

As you walk into the outskirts of the town, there are the shepherds with their flocks of sheep, sitting around the fire, roasting marshmallows and sipping hot chocolate. At the very end of the path stand Bob and I, answering questions and wishing you a Merry Christmas! You'll recognize me. I am the one hugging the chicken.

MOORE MERRIER CHRISTMAS

They say that a family is like a good batch of fudge...sweet and creamy with a few nuts, or in the case of our family, lots of nuts. But that is alright with me. I love nuts!

In the past few years as our family has scattered across the country, our home has become the gathering place at Christmas, where you can get a comfortable bed and a hot meal and reunite with all the nutty relatives. In anticipation, we clean, decorate, cook and buy a huge supply of paper plates, napkins, and cups. The celebration begins when our two SUU students, Taryn and Andrea arrived home, and when they're here we also get sister Katie. She doesn't sleep here anymore, but she does like to come over and cook, so she is always welcome. Around midnight a couple of days later, Karen, Bobby and their two Texas pecans, Brett and Heidi arrive at our front door. Alyse and her husband Dan come from Las Vegas. Dan is the kind of nut everyone should have in their family. He is a *Fix It* nut and bolt guy, and as soon as his bag is unpacked he begins making repairs around the house. He set all the clocks, fixed the singing toilet, and connected the computers with Wi-Fi before bedtime.

Later on, we began our shuttle service to the airport. We picked up Pam who flew in from Virginia, and Dan's mother. Weidmanns have two married sons who live nearby with their three extraordinarily bright and beautiful grandchildren, (our great grandchildren). They come up every day during the holidays so as not to miss any thing fun.

On Christmas Eve and it's time for our traditional family talent show. Karen directs our kazoo band, much to the anxiety of the neighborhood dogs and cats. And this year, Rob and Chelsea's little 18 month old boy, Max, took to the kazoo, like a squirrel to nuts. He hummed away and twirled around in a circle until he fell down on the floor. We all laughed with him, so he decided to do it again...and again...and again. Soon he just put the kazoo in his mouth and fell to the floor cutting out all the twirling. This nut struck a new note in the family.

Rob's daughter, Sophia, surprised us by reading *A Visit From St. Nick,* and she is only four.

Kurt and Kelsey's little girl, Alexandra turns one in a few weeks and takes great delight in showing everyone, "So big!" And she has discovered the soft hair on top of her head, so she gives herself a pat down, and messes up her hair-do.

The Weidmann boys perform an impromptu German slap dance that always ends up in a free for all with everyone like a pile of nuts on the floor.

To close, we tell the Christmas Story and sing carols and head out to the kitchen to eat chocolate.

The little kids get to open one present...soft new pajamas, and it's off to bed.

Dave and Jon stop in from time to time to cook and eat, but they bug out when the noise level gets too high.

I often have trouble sleeping, but Christmas Eve is the worst for me. Bob used to make me stay in bed until it was light enough to see the numbers on the clock, so last year I bought a clock that projects the time on the ceiling He said I was cheating. Now he makes me wait until 7 a.m. Then I turn on all the lights, stoke the fireplace, turn on the Christmas music, and settle into my recliner with a fuzzy blanket to enjoy the show.

We have a bunch of great cooks in the family, and we eat too much, play too hard, laugh 'till we cry, and we stir up many Moore merry memories. What a great Christmas!

BABY HAIR

You know those models on TV who twirl their beautiful hair to show the highlights? Well, that will never be me...nope, nope, no. I took a good hard look at my locks this morning and my hair above my wrinkled brow looks pretty much like it did when I was a toddler. It's mousy brown, fine, and thin. When I was four years old I had a pesky little bald cousin, who used to chase me around to touch my hair. My mother would say, "Let Jane feel your hair. She doesn't have much of her own." Feel, schmeel; she was only two and she didn't just feel. She grabbed my hair and tried to pull it out! But life is not fair and when she finally did grow her own hair, it was beautifully blond and naturally curly. Wouldn't you know it? Aunt Marba, Jane's mother used to brush it around her finger and make lovely Shirley Temple curls. Then she tried that with my hair. This was before curlers, so she would wet my head, brush the wet curls around her finger and secure them with a bobby pin. It took lots of time, and unless I had a book to distract me, I got restless and began to wiggle. That would cause Marba to smack me on top of the head with the hair brush and all my curls would come loose and we'd have to start all over again.

When I was a teenager, Mom decided a perm was just what my fine hair needed. She took me to a small beauty shop in Provo where they still used one of those perm machines that fried the curl into your hair. It resembled and upside down mixing bowl, with wires like octopus arms, and cooking clips on the end. After my hair was all done up, they turned on the electricity until the hair smoked . Then they put my cooked curls in bobby pins, and I sat under the giant beehive dryer until my ears turned red. They styled my hair, and I was ready for the world. I must admit it looked pretty good...the first day. But the next morning it turned into major frizz, and I looked like the Jackson Five, all on one little mousy head. Trying to get a comb through it was pure torture.

About this same time the beauty gurus came out with a little marvel called *hair spray.* It came in one flavor, Toni Super Hold. With my thin locks, every hair has to be in its own special place, and this stuff worked. It was really more like glue, and once on your hair, it stuck there until death or a good scrubbing, which ever came first.

When I went off to college, my room mate Shauna and I experimented with hair colors. First we decided to be blondes to see if they did have more fun. So out came the peroxide bottle, and we looked stunning. After a few months, we needed a change and decided that raven black locks might be just the look for us. We were cautious though, and just bought temporary black dye in case we didn't like it. We did everything according to instructions, and when we took the towels off, our hair had turned *dark green.* Our friends were writhing on the floor laughing and Shauna and I ran for the nearest beauty shop. We were able to get in before closing time, and after the stylists stopped giggling they redyed us brown, with green highlights.

After that, my hair stayed unpermed and undyed until after I was married. We were living in California and had Karen and baby Dave. Bob was going to night school, and was involved in church work, so I was home alone with the kids and the dog most of the time. After they were in bed I needed a project, so I decided a new hair color would brighten my life. I discovered *henna.* It is a wonderful hair product, but it can vary in color from deep auburn to bright orange, and sure enough; one day I ended up with bright orange hair. I don't discourage easily, so I just bought one of the new synthetic wigs and waited for my orange mouse fuzz to grow out again.

My biggest hair disaster happened in Salt Lake about 20 years ago, while we were visiting Pam who was then married with three girls of her own. She had a special hair dresser from Puerto Rico who looked all of 16, but had a cult of loyal followers. He looked down his nose at my locks and asked, "Have chew ever tried extensions, Darlin? If chew will let my people work on you, ve vill put your picture in the paper!" I never could turn down an adventure, so we began. It took from 9 a.m. until 8 p.m. as they burned each little segment of new hair onto each little segment of my own hair. When one person would get tired of working on me, another one would show up, and I sat, and sat, and sat. Finally the boss came over and did a little hair styling and face make up, and said I looked just like Joan Crawford of *Mommy Dearest* movie fame. He sent me out to a photographer for pictures and they were in Sunday's paper, to the amusement of my relatives, who never thought I'd be a hair model.

The next morning I got up, looked in the mirror in broad daylight, and started to cry. My head looked like one of those Barbie Dolls with little holes and tufts of hair poking out all over. We had to go back home to Cedar City, and during the ride home I pulled and broke those things out of my hair. When I had finished, most of my hair was about an inch long and completely nonexistent in some places. I had to teach school the next morning, so I tied a scarf around my head and reported for work. I looked like a sun bleached Aunt Jemima. After school I hurried over to my trusted hair dresser, and she said, "What *have* you done now?" She evened things up as best she could, but suggested I use a good conditioner and get a wig until my hair grew out again. Never trust 16 year old Puerto Ricans with your hair.

Needless to say, now I have a wonderful collection of wigs, falls, wiglets, and hair extensions all in radiant red. If any of you need help, my collection and I are available. Contact me at gotwigs.com.

FAMILY PORTRAIT

Every five years or so, I become very matriarchal and want to have a family portrait made for all the world to admire. And every five years or so, it becomes a family battle of wits. And every five years or so Bob always starts out with, "To get 26 of us in the same place at the same time is like trying to push a rope." Then Dave, age 49 says, "I'm not going to get a haircut or shave." And Brett, age 13 says, "I'm not going to wear the same color as the girls," and the battle begins.

The last time the entire family posed was in 1999 on our front porch in Highland, just before Rob was to leave for his mission. We all wore blue denim which was fine for everyone except Brett, who was just four. His choice of attire were his new Superman pj's with an red shiny cape. His mother finally did talk him into denims *over* his pj's, but only after the photographer had taken special shots of him flying down the stairs.

Then when the urge hit me in 2004, Bob talked me into having small group shots taken and then we could put them into a nice arrangement on top of the TV. So the Weidmanns in Texas, all put on Hawaiian shirts and shorts and posed with their bare feet hanging out. In Utah, Bob, David, Jon, Rob, Chelsea (Rob's wife) and I all posed in beautiful shades of red and orange fall colors, but kept our shoes on. No matter how much I begged and pleaded, Pam wouldn't have her family picture taken. Finally the girls, Taryn, Andrea, and Katie, took matters into their own hands and had a beautiful picture taken of the three of them out in the snow, with their boots on.

This year I made the executive decision to wear green and/or blue, and since I don't like conflict I adopted an "anything goes" attitude. We made several trips to the thrift store, and Andrea,

65

who has a style of her own, found a royal blue silk blouse with bat-wing sleeves and a blue elastic belt. Others found cool blue and green shirts. Daniel (Alyse's husband) arrived at the airport in a bright green suit with matching vest that he had made for him while on his mission in El Salvador. He resembled a very tall leprechaun with a suitcase. Alyse wore a gorgeous lime green silk skirt and blouse. Bob opted for a navy blue shirt, and I wore the same color. After all, 54 years of marriage does give me that option.

So all attired properly, off we went to the park to meet the photographer at the bridge. The only big problem was the wind. It was a good thing Andrea was wearing an elastic belt so we could snap her back in place when the wind caught in her bat-winged sleeves. I wore my new "touch of gray" wig that I had stapled to my head so the wind wouldn't snatch it off. Our three little great-grandkids, Sophia (3), Max (6 months), and Alexandra (1 month) were wonderful. The wind would catch their breath and make them giggle. Pam was in Iowa and couldn't come home for a picture, so I had her face photo-shopped into the group. She is the only one who's hair isn't flying around.

Karen, unbeknown to her parents, had made a sign for the front of the group that said, *Rent-A-Family.Com.* I noticed that several strange people lined up, and were handing Karen money. I wondered if any of them were going to come to our family dinner that afternoon.

After the photo shoot, we all went back to our condo for a birthday party...my 75th. We had lots of food, balloons, flowers, and my favorite triple chocolate cake with sparklers and enough candles to set off the fire alarm. Now I'm a happy little matriarch, for the next five years or so.

By the way...we used that picture on our Christmas card, and Stan called to say, "I loved your family picture, but why didn't you put the names on it so I would know who they are?"

Bob sez, "I don't know who they are. We just rented them for the day!"

TRAVELING WITH KIDS

When our three kids were still in school and Bob and I were both teaching, we decided it would be fun to travel together and see the good old USA. We'd all save our money in a big red piggy bank and as soon a school was out for the summer, we would load the camper, motor home, or whatever, and off we'd go. Traveling with three kids is like being pecked to death by a duck. We endured a lot of pecky situations, but bruised and battered, we all made it home in time for school in the fall.

David, our son, recalls our third summer of travels together:

Summer and our suitcases (or in Dad's case...brown grocery bags) were practically packing themselves in anticipation of our annual summer adventure. Which adventure it was, and to what coordinates on the map, I do not recall, nor is it relevant now. As the last days of school crawled painfully along, every single one just barely pulling itself past by the skin of its fingernails, the members of our family began to get what is known in the recreational medicine discipline as "Kampgrounds Of America on the brain;" a condition where every last thought is in some way connected with National Parks and a bubble-leveling camper. We were ready to embark. We had been eating, sleeping, and drooling vacation, planning how we would pick each other up in the camper on the last day of school, thus saving valuable vacation time by not having to go home first and change clothing. Then, fate threw a monkey wrench into our propane-propelled plans. Dad got a hernia.

"Darn him," we cried. "How could he do this to our vacation?" Our first reaction of course, was just to leave him at home and take off across the country without him. "Hitch hike to Virginia, and we'll meet you there," I suggested. That wasn't feasible, of course...who in the world would give a ride to a strange man in a hospital gown? So we considered inviting our friend, the surgeon to come along: He could do the operation at a rest stop! I think it was Mom who came up with the final solution: "Get your little operation taken care of during finals week, so that the day after school lets out, we can put you in the camper and go."

"Yeh, and no whimpering," was Karen's comment, I think.

Well now, that solution sounded agreeable to at least four of us, so the matter was settled. A week before we were ready to leave, Dad went under the knife. We gave him a week to recuperate or change his mind and stay at home...we'd send plenty of postcards. Bent over and slow, we borrowed a refrigerator dolly and loaded him into the bed above the cab and made vapor trails down the highway.

It was rough going at first. We didn't know if we were allowed to leave fathers locked inside the vehicles while we visited amusement parks, or if we had to pay full price for him at campgrounds, or did they offer a special "invalid rate," or if there was any sort of painkiller we might administer to keep him from making so much noise when we drove over bumps. And none of us knew the first thing about removing stitches. Pam kept trying to feed him her famous bread balls, with cheese inside, but Dad insisted they gummed up his works. He survived the first few weeks out though, and finally got well enough to limp along behind us through all the tourist attractions. Eventually, he was able to even hit a few speed bumps of his own as he took over the driving.

All said and done, we were glad he was able to accompany us on vacation that year and pay for things. At least he didn't have to stay home in bed with only our dog Abby and his misery for company.

Seniors on the Go

We love to go when we can. Been there. Done that. Can't remember, so we do it all again.

ADVENTURES IN AIR TRAVEL

I would like to put an end to a nasty rumor that is circulating. I did *not* fall in love with flying when I saw Orville Wright take off in his flying machine in 1903. I did *not* ask to ride with him, and as far as I know the only passengers on that plane were a couple of pigeons who were trying to get out of the wind. My first airplane ride was in 1957, when Bob was still a student at BYU. My parents sent me and baby Karen (age one) an airline ticket to Ely, Nevada so we could come visit them. The plane was the latest four-prop engine model that was so loud your ears rang hours later. In the olden days, the people who flew on airplanes looked like they could afford a ticket, and dressed in their best, which included gloves and a proper hat for the ladies. The stewardesses (as they were called) wore fancy uniforms and perky little hats atop their puffy hair. They earned their keep serving drinks and a semi-delicious hot meal with real dishes and silverware with the airline logo on it. And then there was another drink before reaching your destination. By the time we walked down the stairs onto the tarmac, Karen needed a diaper change and I needed the bathroom. My parents were waiting in the lounge with flowers for me and balloons for Karen, and I loved flying!

Now fifty years later, the attack of 9-11 has changed flying dramatically. People dress so casually they sometimes look like they wore the first thing they found on the floor that morning. There is no more waiting in a comfortable lounge with your friends. The security checks are scary. First you have to shed your carry-on bags, jacket, and your shoes, and put them in a tray that goes through an x-ray machine. Salt Lake airport has a puffer. You stand in a little glass booth and they puff air up your skirt to see if you're hiding explosives in your underwear. The lines are long and the people get grumpy, especially the ones wearing the badges. I've even had to submit to the dreaded wand a few times. Does a chubby little old lady look like a terrorist? I was tempted to say, "This roll around my middle is fat, not explosives," but I kept my mouth shut and just giggled. The wand lady didn't look like she had a sense of humor, and I wasn't about to make her mad. Besides, she was wearing a burka.

Flying still has its share of adventure. A few years ago we were headed to Dallas, and then on to Midland to visit Karen and her family. Suddenly the pilot announced that we would be making an unscheduled landing in Houston. They had been trying to fly around a huge storm and were running low on fuel. Now if our luggage hadn't been held hostage on the plane we could have rented a car right there and driven to Midland. But instead we got back on the plane like good little passengers, and off we went into the wild blue yonder. That storm was centered over Dallas, so between down drafts the pilot put the plane onto the tarmac. But by then there were no gates available. So we sat on the runway, strapped in our seats while the wind rocked the plane back and forth until I turned a lovely shade of green. I swallowed some motion sickness pills without water, because all of the snacks and drinks we gone, and held on to Bob for dear life.

Just as we finished writing our will on the back of an airsickness bag, the plane was able to get to a gate and we all got off and rushed to the bathrooms. Then things got bad! All the flights in and out of Dallas had been canceled, all the hotels in the area were full, and there was not a rental car available for any price. The man at the service desk gave us a small pillow and a blanket big enough to cover our arms, and a kit with toothbrush, paste, soap, and a razor, in case we wanted to slit our wrists. At 10 p.m. all the food courts and and shops closed down leaving hundreds of stranded passengers just wandering around. Bob found a nice place on the floor in a corner, and curled up with his blanket over his shoulders and went right to sleep. That man can sleep anywhere.

I tried the floor, but it hurt my back. Two big husky men turned a row of seats around to face another row, and planted their backsides on one row and their feet on the other. I tried that too, but my short legs wouldn't reach. Finally I discovered where they parked the carts that they used to haul old people around, and found that I could curl up on the front seat under the steering wheel, and that's where I spent the night trying to put myself into sleep mode.

When the sun woke up, so did the passengers, and the shops opened to a booming business. The lines for breakfast were long and slow, but I did manage to grab a bagel and juice before we boarded our American Eagle prop-plane to Midland. We sat there for a long time munching our breakfast but going no where, when what should come bouncing across the tarmac but *my* sleeping cart and a mechanic on board with his tool belt flapping in the wind. He got to our plane, opened up the cowling on one engine, and smacked it with his hammer. He turned and gave a thumbs up to the pilot and we took off. Bob settled back into his seat and went to sleep, while I willed that airplane up in the air for the 45 minutes it took to reach Midland, and after all that I still love to fly!

BOB'S KOREAN TALE

In honor of Veteran's Day Bob tells this tale of his first heroic days in Korea.

In 1950 when my class graduated from Provo High School, we hadn't intended to save the world from communism. We were much more interested in who had the coolest car, and who was dating the cutest girl. But then North Korea ruined it all by invading South Korea, and where in the heck was Korea anyway? I was not anxious to be drafted into the Army and sleep in a fox hole, so I enlisted in the Air Force. Besides I liked the look of Air Force blues. I reported to Ft. Douglas for my physical and was inducted into the United States Air Force in February 1951.

I sold my beloved Mercury convertible, kissed my family and girlfriend Jeannie goodbye, and headed into the sunset to save the world from the communist threat.

When I finished basic training and school for repair and maintenance of aerial reconnaissance cameras, the Air Force told me there was some good news and some bad.   The good news was that after I served at a foreign base for a year, I could be stationed at any air base of my choice. The bad news was, that the foreign base was Kimpo Air Base at Seoul, Korea.

After ten days at sea on a troop ship, a plane flew me from Japan to my base in Korea. We landed, they opened the door, and I peered out on pure desolation. The city had been repeatedly bombed, and nothing was standing over four feet tall. I said, "Whoa...this was not in my enlistment agreement!" They just shoved me out the door and threw my duffel bag out after me.

Everything on the air base was under extremely tight security. A tough North Korean general had sworn an oath to be in control of Kimpo within a month. I was handed a rifle and ammunition, and hustled to a tent just off the runway. Inside were all the comforts of home: a pot belly stove, canvas cots, a wooden footlocker, and five other confused and frightened guys, all liberally coated with white DDT powder to control the bugs. I had arrived in hell just in time for indoctrination. We were warned to be prepared for an invasion or sneak attack anytime. Enemy infiltrators liked to sneak into our tents in the dark of night and kill the UN peace keepers as they slept. So much for keeping peace.

I had a hard time getting to sleep that night, and when I finally did, an air raid siren screamed through my dreams. I jumped out of bed, found my pants, slipped into my boots without tying them, and grabbed my rifle. My tent mate, Allen, shouted, "Moore...turn on the flashlight!"

"I can't do that. Those commies will know where we are."

"Moore...turn on the damn flashlight. I can't get my pants on, damn it!"

"No!"

"MOORE!"

I shaded the light with my hand and shined it on Allen. There he was, trying to shove his leg into his laundry bag. "Oh, damn," he said and grabbed his boots and rifle, and headed out into the dark in his shorts. There hadn't been time at Kimpo to dig trenches so our best defense was into the rice paddy.

I knew I was in trouble with my first step into the mud. My boots came off and I fell face first, catching myself with my hands and my rifle. "Wait," I yelled, as I felt around in the muck for my boots. With my muddy boots in one hand and my muddy rifle in my other, I made it up to a little hill with two other airmen. What do airmen know about ground combat anyway?

We took stock of our resources. I had pants, muddy boots, and a rifle full of muck. Allen had no pants, a clean rifle, but no bullets. Our other companion Lange, had pants, boots, no rifle, but he did have his lucky bullet in his pocket. We gave the bullet to Allen for his rifle, and he stood guard over us as we shivered in the cold night air.

The sirens blared away, and a little old biplane appeared over the horizon. The anti-aircraft guns lit up the night sky trying to shoot him down, but he just flew too slowly. He came over the base, leaned out of the cockpit and dropped his one small bomb by hand. It came crashing down into the garbage dump and then he flew off into the night. Later we learned that he came over frequently just to interrupt our sleep, and we dubbed him Bedcheck Charlie. I spent a year at Kimpo and I'm happy to say that Bedcheck Charlie never again caught us with our pants down.

GO IN THE GENERAL DIRECTION

In this age of electronic goodies such as GPS and Map Quest, there are still some die hards that like to head off in the *general direction* when they go somewhere, and the ones I'm acquainted with are in the Moore family.

We went on a day trip with brother Stan and Carol. The four of us had been to a funeral in Springville, and we went out to lunch to celebrate the fact that the funeral was not for any of us. We were in the vicinity of the Stouffer's frozen food outlet, and if there's anything I love, it's frozen food meals. All I have to do is stick them in the microwave and Voila! Dinner! Well now, we could see our target building from the road, so we headed in the *general direction*. We drove through a beautiful industrial park with fountains, giant trees, walkways, picnic benches, and duck heaven. There were, by my count 327.5 ducks of various species and gender, and there were countless sparrows and pigeons hanging around the premises looking for a free handout from the lunches of the office workers. We drove out of the park and after a few twists and turns in the road, we got a whiff of stinky air, that was coming from the direction we were headed. As we turned the corner there was the sewage processing plant in all its smelly glory. We all moaned at Stan, but he assured us that he knew that Stouffer's was in this *general direction*, and we kept going on down the road. We passed cows in a pasture chewing their cud, and across the street was a field full of sheep chewing up the grass. The bushes kept getting taller, and the trees higher, and soon all we could see was green and greener. Then we turned the corner and lo and behold, we had arrived at Stouffer's, and Stan was laughing at us.

A few weeks ago Bob and I had been at the Jordon River Temple, and afterwards planned to head north to a store that advertised a complete 72 hour survival kit for two people, all in a nice handy back pack. We thought that would be the very thing to have during the next big Utah tornado, so off we went. We got as far as 30th South, but no store. So with much mumbling and grumbling Bob decided to ask directions. The man said, "Oh, that store is over on State Street, not Redwood Road," and so we turned and headed east in the *general direction*. But the great city of Salt Lake has a freeway that runs north and south with just a few select bridges underneath. We traveled down dead end streets, and around some cul de sacs, and as we turned one corner we drove right smack into the parking lot of this lovely gold-domed Muslim mosque. It was beautiful, but we didn't think they'd give tours to infidels, so we flipped a u-turn, and headed in the direction of Redwood Road, wherever the heck that was. We did finally make it to State Street, got our back pack, and headed home in the *general direction*.

Years earlier we owned a brand new red motor boat, and decided to take Bob's parents for a ride on Utah Lake. The only recognizable feature in the lake is a place in the southeast called Bird Island, because of the birds that like to picnic there. So off we sailed in the *general direction*. Just as Bob was saying, "It must be close," we heard a terrible crunch, and our boat came to rest on top of Bird Island. Someone had forgotten to tell us that the water was high that year, and Bird Island was under the water. Bob got out and pushed the boat off the island, but the encounter had massacred the propeller on our cute little boat. We slowly paddled back to shore, and I'm sure I saw smoke coming out of Bob's ears.

In a month from now we are heading out to cruise through the Panama Canal. On my map the Canal is southeast of here, but we are not going that direction...no, no, nope. We are going northwest to board the ship in Vancouver. That is not even in the *general direction* at all, so if you don't hear from me during September...not to worry. I'll be somewhere between the Atlantic and Pacific ocean.

FALL FROM MT. OLYMPUS

Over many years, Bob and I have learned to travel light, but traveling without any luggage at all, is a whole different myth. We were bound for a Mexican Riviera cruise in 1988, aboard the Goddess of the Sea. It began with a flight out of Los Angeles to La Paz, Mexico where our ship was docked. Bob has a penchant for being an hour early for any flight, and this was before the 9-11 security screenings. The only problem getting to the airplane gate in those days, was trying to dodge the Hare Krishnas beating their tambourines and passing out flowers.

We stayed at a hotel near the airport, and parked our car at the back of the lot, hoping it wouldn't be noticed for a week. We took the shuttle into LAX and checked our bags. Bob settled in with his books while I shopped. The airplane was on time, and off we flew to Mexico. We boarded the ship about noon, and went up to find lunch at the buffet as we set sail away on the waters of Poseidon in the sea of Cortez. When we got back to our room, there was no luggage for us. Off we went to the purser's desk, and he said, "Not to worry. Your luggage will be here by dinner time." We sat on the deck for a while and then went in and had a nice dinner, but still no luggage.

I was frantically going through my purse, looking for lipstick and any other makeup, but it was slim pickin's. It was back to the purser. This time there was a small crowd of 27 unhappy travelers, and it was time to panic. A very nervous purser told us they were checking on the luggage and would have information for us after the evening show. We all grumbled our way through the festivities, and hustled back to the purser. Now it just so happened that within this Lost Luggage Group, (LLG as we were now called) there was a contract negotiator and he was big and he was **loud**. Like Thor he thundered, **"What are you going to do about our luggage!"**

The trembling little purser murmured, "We've sent out a tracer."

"And what are we supposed to do until you find it? Run around naked?" Sounded like a good idea to me. I'd just lost 20 pounds. All of us minions were cheering on our negotiator.

"I don't know what to do," said the purser, looking like he'd been struck by lightning.

"Then find someone who does," he roared and we all stood our ground.

Finally the captain came down and offered us all $100 credit at the ship's store. It was a very small store with large prices, so the credit was not going to buy much. We got toothbrushes, cosmetics, razor, flip flops, and a windbreaker. One large lady from New York was looking through a box of women's lacy panties. She looked at me and said, "I don't wear this kind of underwear...do you?"

"Absolutely not," I answered truthfully. Bob and I had washed our underwear and dried it with the hair dryer that night.

The next day we still didn't have our luggage, but we were having LLG group meetings and our fearless leader had gotten us $50 a day at the store until our luggage was returned safely. By the time our stipend ran out we were buying gifts for all the family.

Two days later was the big formal night and the LLG got creative. After all, these were special circumstances. We borrowed bed sheets and made togas, fastened at the shoulder with plastic grapes from the buffet decor, and wore a garlands of leaves we borrowed from the artificial plants on board the ship. We looked like demented Greek gods. But when we got to the dining room the head waiter politely and firmly said we were not dressed appropriately and sent us up to the buffet for dinner. I wanted to smite him with a mighty lightning bolt.

After four days they located our luggage and the LLG cheered as it was ferried out from shore and brought on board. It was like your best friend returning from Hades. That night the captain had a special formal party for the LLG with caviar and champagne, neither of which I like, so I feasted on soda pop and chip dip. Apparently our luggage cart had been loaded on the wrong airplane and it had been all the way to Machu Pichu and back. It had been opened and searched. I had packed a plastic bag full of Metamucil in my case and it had been slit open and all my clothes were covered in it. Fortunately, it brushed out easily and provided nice fiber for the carpet in our cabin.

The last day of the cruise, the captain called the LLG together and said, "Although it was not our fault, we realize your cruise was not the best, so we're presenting you all with a free cruise you can take within the next two years." Bob and I decided that five days without luggage was a small price to pay for another cruise.

SWAMP THINGS

A new TV show appeared on the History Channel called *Swamp People,* and it reminded me of my youth, with Pogo in the Okefenokee Swamp. He was a cartoon character with his pals Albert Alligator and Mam'selle Hepzibah, and I loved them all. Bob and I were traveling through Florida a few years back and saw the Okefenokee Swamp road and off we went on another adventure. I expected to see cute lil' creatures like Bun Rab, and Howland Owl, but as we drove in all we saw were herds of deer being bugged by swarms of mosquitoes. We arrived at the visitor's center where there were wooden walkways around so you could observe the swamp from all angles. The ranger told us if we really wanted to see wild life we could rent a boat and go off into the swamp by ourselves. Yessah, that was for me. I always wanted to be a swamp witch. Trouble was, Bob did not have the same magic vision. Instead of renting a power boat which was more money, he rented a dugout canoe that sat down deep in the water closer to the alligators. If he was trying to scare me, he did a good job of it. After a liberal spraying of mosquito repellent, he put me in the bow of the boat like bait, and off we went in search of Pogo and his assorted friends.

Bob rowed along, and except for the sound of frogs, and the buzz of insects it was very quiet. Then he whispered, "Do you see that?"

"Do I see what," sez I.

"Alligator eyes looking for lunch." Sure enough...there by the roots of a tree were two big yellow eyes staring at little juicy me, and as we went past, that 'gator just silently sunk down in the water out of sight. Although the water was too murky to see anything, I just knew he was following us, waiting to capsize the boat and eat me. Bob just kept on rowing and we saw birds, deer, and turtles, and when our hour was up, we headed back to the dock and I jumped out and ran as fast as I could to the car before I became someone's snack. So much for Pogo and his cute friends.

A few years later we were with Mona and Harold, and we allowed that it might be fun to ride through the swamp in an air boat with the big engine in back. They could outrun any gator, couldn't they?   So at the next turn off, Bob drove down a hill to the river. There stood two swamp buggies at the dock and they looked fine, but the rest of the scenery was like something right out of *Deliverance.* There was an old shack built on stilts over the water, with Granny sitting in a dilapidated rocker smoking her corn cob pipe, watching two skinny little kids playing in the dirt. She was surrounded by homemade fishing poles, a sleepy ol' hound dog too lazy to bark, and a whole porch packed with cases of beer.

Mona and I were livid. "Why did you pick this place out in the middle of nowhere?" we demanded.

Bob said, "They had a nice handmade sign for swamp tours that looked economical."

We happened to be driving a forest green Cadillac that I had inherited from my father, and the swamp crew had their eyes on that car. Mona and I were not about to get out.

"Oh, come on. Let's see what they charge for a tour. It'll be fun!" Yeah, fun schmun. They'll dump our bodies out in the swamp for the alligators to eat and trade our car in for more beer.

Bob and Harold got out and met Bubba and Claudine, and decided that an hour tour wouldn't be fatal. They dragged Mona and I down and put us into the boat. I waved a fond farewell to my beautiful car, and we were off. We'd only gone about two miles when the boat coughed and died. I thought *this is it! This is where they push us into the water*, and I grabbed Mona's hand. But Claudine said, "Don't worry, ya'll. I'll call Bubba on the radio and he'll be right out with the other boat." And sure 'nuff, in a few minutes here comes Bubba. We crawled into his boat and were off again. This time we saw some huge gators sunning themselves on the bank, but they were scared of our big noisy boat and hustled away with surprising agility. As Pogo said, "We have met the enemy and he is us."

In spite of all my fears, it turned out to be quite a nice trip, and I resisted the urge to kiss the hood of my car when we got back. They didn't offer us a beer, but Bubba and Claudine both hoisted a cold one as we drove away. I did notice that Mona's hand was a bit bruised.

OUR MINUTE OF FAME

Andy Warhol said, "In the future, everyone will be famous for 15 minutes." Bob and I have already had ours. Well okay, it was more like 15 seconds of fame, and we had to be in a ship wreck to do it. We were in that famous ship wreck in Buzzard Bay, just off the coast of Plymouth, Massachusetts in 1987. You remember, don't you? It was in the newspapers and on CNN, for one whole day.

In case you missed it, this is the story from an eye witness...me. It all began on a nice little cruise that left New York harbor, sailed up the east coast and down the St. Lawrence seaway to Montreal. At least that was what they'd advertised. We stayed in New York the first night, and in the morning they took us to the Star Liner Ship. As we sailed away we waved to the Statue of Liberty, who is actually a lovely shade of sea sick green.

All was well that night, and the next morning we were scheduled to go through the Cape Cod Canal. Bob and I got up early to walk the deck. It was foggy, but being on a ship we thought there was no problem getting lost, so off we went. We could see the sun through the fog, and noticed the ship was going around in circles. We figured they were probably waiting for the fog to lift so we would have a good view of the Canal.

We finished our walk, and went down to the dining room for breakfast. Everything was in order, including the waiters who were there with our orange juice and toast. All of a sudden there was an ear-splitting screech, and all of the ship's personnel disappeared leaving us with our spoons in mid air. The ship came to a dead stop, and we were in for a new adventure.

Everyone hurried out on deck, and there were passengers and crew all hanging their heads over the rail to watch fuel bubbling up from under the ship...not a good sign. Soon a couple of tug boats chugged over and laid out floats to keep the fuel from spreading, although the rainbow colors on the water were beautiful.

The tugs got on one side of the ship and pushed. Nothing. Then they got on the other side and pushed. Nothing. Then one got on the starboard front and the other got on the port back and tried to twist us off the rocks. Still nothing! By this time the fog had lifted and hundreds of small boats had come out to see the ship wreck. There were even helicopters circling overhead. Bob and I were smiling and waving to everyone. We could see land on three sides and since we were both good swimmers, we figured we could swim if necessary.

At noon the ship's captain finally came to the conclusion that we were definitely *stuck* on the rocks. They put out all the food and drinks and invited everyone to party hardy. And I did. I drank five Cokes with my lunch and then went to our cabin to go to the bathroom, pack, go to the bathroom, get ready to abandon ship, and go to the bathroom.

They sent out several small ferries, took off all the luggage, and then the passengers. As we left the ship, they gave us big sack lunches with sandwiches, fruit and a six pack of Coke.

We sailed to a pier outside of Boston where buses were waiting, and we rode into the city to a fancy hotel. The next morning they called us into a big conference room. There sat our luggage. It was a little damp from the morning rain, but by that time I was just glad to get a change of undies. They told us to collect our luggage and arranged for us to get out of town on the next available plane. They even refunded all of our money. The rocks had torn a hole in the ship 2 feet by 90 feet, but they floated it off the rocks at high tide and into the harbor for repairs. It must have taken a long time because I haven't heard of Star Liner ships since.

It was great fun, but I was anxious to call the kids and tell them we were safe. Pam said, "We knew that, Mom. We watched you and Dad get off the ferry and onto the bus. You were on CNN!" I'm so glad I wore bright red for my 15 seconds of fame!

RIDING THE RAILS

There is a fancy new train in town that runs from Salt Lake to Ogden, along the Wasatch front, and is called aptly enough, *Front Runner.* I wanted to ride that new train, so I appointed myself tour director and called Stan and Carol. They were in the mood for a new day trip, so off we went. Stan drove us up to the TRAX station at Sandy, and while Bob and Stan figured out how to buy bulletos from a very grimy machine, Carol and I walked up to the TRAX door and pushed the button to get on. Since I was the director, but slower than the other three, I climbed on, found four nice seats and plopped down. All of a sudden a feminine voice cooed, "This train will be leaving shortly," and that darn train moved out, leaving Bob, Stan, Carol, and the tickets standing at the depot. Then the voice added guilt to my lost feeling, and said, "You must have proof of payment when requested." I had no ticket! It was in Bob's hand back in Sandy. I shrunk down into the corner of my seat and tried to make myself as inconspicuous as possible. TRAX people do not appreciate freeloaders, but then they do not check tickets on every ride either. Who would suspect a nice little old lady like moi?

I pulled out my cell phone and called Carol. She said, "Don't panic...just get off at the Gallivan Center and wait for us to catch up with you. We'll be on the next train. And by the way, you're fired as our tour director."

Well, I waited at the Gallivan Center and met every incoming train, and they did finally come after about 20 minutes. Bob said, "Aren't you embarrassed trying to ditch us?" I put on my humble demeanor and we all rode TRAX to the hub, and there waiting for us was a beautiful sleek two-story *Front Runner* train. We headed over to the ticket booth to buy $6 tickets to Ogden. All around the depot there were stacks of luggage, brief cases and paper bags. "This really looks junky," sez me. But on closer inspection, I discovered they were sculptures...modern art, if you will. You can't beat that. They were so appropriate for a transportation hub.

We boarded the train, climbed up to the highest level, and sat down in nice plush seats with head rests. It was elegant and clean, and I kept waiting for someone to come around with drinks and snacks. The ride was smooth and quiet with only two stops. It seemed slow, but when I looked out at the freeway, we were passing all the cars, and speeding right along. Bob and Stan caught up on their talking and I found myself nodding off to sleep. After all, it was nap time and I'd had a difficult morning.

The station at Ogden was only three blocks from down town. Just a block south of the depot was the Utah State Railroad Museum. The buildings were old but nicely refurbished. Inside we also found the Browning Firearms Museum, the Browning-Kimball Car Museum, and an excellent restaurant. After lunch we lost Bob and Stan with the firearms, so Carol and I headed for the gift shop. The Moore men, knowing how much we can spend in a gift shop, cut their visit short and herded us over to the antique cars. I like antiques because I am one. I especially enjoyed the model train that took up the entire north end of the building. It had towns, farms, prairies and purple mountain's majesty. I like miniatures too, because I am one.

It took us about three hours to see everything before we came back to Salt Lake on the Front Runner and then TRAX to Sandy. There was one last snag. When we got to the Sandy Station, Stan had a senior moment, and forgot where he parked the car. So after wandering around like little old lost sheep, he pushed the panic button on his key ring, found the beeping, blinking car and drove us home.

ROAD TRIP

Every five years or so, my Bob goes through a type of male menopause that can only be cured by the purchase of a new (to us) car. He had one of his spells in August, and with his *Consumer's Guide* clutched in his hand, he covered all the used car dealerships from Orem to Bountiful. He doesn't invite me along at first, and when he comes home he spends hours making copious notes and mumbling to himself. Then when he figures he's done enough research, he takes me along kicking and complaining to visit the two finalists in his quest. By then, he usually has his mind made up and I just become a "yes" man. This year the winner was a nice little pearl white Toyota Solara with excellent gas mileage.

Well now, let's figure this out. If you get a new car with excellent gas mileage, it's time to test it out by going on a road trip...right? We have not been on a road trip by ourselves since we were young and in our late sixties. But there is nothing like a senior's road trip to put a little color in life.

We decided to pay a visit to the presidents on Mr. Rushmore in South Dakota. Bob appointed himself tour director and sat down at the computer and planned everything out using Price Line and Map Quest. He graciously allowed me a week to prepare. Since we weren't flying we didn't need to conserve on luggage space, and we went a bit overboard in an effort to fill our new trunk. Bob had his clothes bag, and I had mine, and there were big bags of electronic stuff; my DVD player, camera, and six CD books for our listening pleasure. I had my drawing supplies and a big bag of snacks. Bob wanted to take healthy fruits and veggies and I added crackers, cheese sticks, and nuts. It was a great plan, except we had a senior moment and drove off leaving all the healthy food in the refrigerator.

Our first day was a 306 mile stretch to Casper, Wyoming. Bob allowed us a two minute bathroom break in the morning, and promised a twenty five minute lunch break at an undisclosed time, mainly because Bob has a hard time stopping the car to eat. Eating is not important to him, and by the time he does stop I am in dire distress and ready to eat anything, even road kill. But with our tummies finally full we push on to the scheduled motel where we hauled in the luggage, and ate cinnamon rolls and milk before bed.

Since the next day was a short drive to Hill City, we made two stops on the way. One was Jewel Cave with 700 steps up and down. My knees, full of cortisone, marched right along, but my asthma kicked in and Bob thought he might have to pack me out on his 76 year old back. But I hobbled slowly along and finally made it into the sunlight again.

The other stop was in Custer National Park. With my active imagination I tried to see ghosts of Indians and Custer in fierce battle, but the ranger informed me that the Battle of Little Big Horn was fought in Montana, not South Dakota. So what, ghosts don't travel? I had to be satisfied seeing the buffalo, elk, deer, eagles and hawks.

Early next morning we headed out to visit George, Thomas, Theodore, and Abraham. They have really fancied up the place since we were last there in 1976. We had a problem getting lost in the big new parking area which was not on our Map Quest, and we kept driving around and circles and coming through the entrance gate several times, before we got it right. We finally got parked and strolled hand in hand up to the big gate bridge. We passed the shops and went down the avenue of state flags to the overlook, and there were those four magnificent faces. Gutzon Borglum was the son of Mormon immigrants. I don't know if he had time for church with all that stone work he was doing, but he certainly did accomplish something magnificent. I happened to notice that the presidents now have lights hanging down their noses and in their hair. I assumed that the lights are for the evening show, and not just to keep them warm in the winter.

I was impressed by the museum, probably because it contained things I recognized from my younger days. It has been modernized with TV and interactive displays. One had a dynamite plunger that you can push and watch the mountain blow up. That was my favorite thing, until some school kid asked me to move so he could have a turn.

Before coming home, we saw the Crazy Horse Monument, Deadwood City, Devil's Tower, and Yellowstone National Park, but those are all stories in themselves. The best part of this road trip was that we still could do it. And the car averaged 36 mpg. Now Bob can rest in peace for another five years, and by then we might be more comfortable driving Jazzy chairs.

THANKFUL FOR TEXAS

We love to spend Thanksgiving in Midland, Texas. Why in Midland, the arm pit of Texas, you well may ask? It's dry, dusty and so flat that you can stand on a tin can and watch your dog run away for two days. Besides, the water tastes bad and the occasional whiff of gas from the oil wells pumping all around makes it stinky. I wonder if taking all that oil from the ground will leave a big void that will eventually collapse and Midland will become choice water front property on the Gulf of Mexico?

They do have hundreds of beautiful birds in Midland, but we go there because of the people...most especially Karen, Bobby with Heidi and Brett, the two offspring who are currently living at home. The two oldest sons, Rob and Kurt, have repented of their Texas ways, and have moved back to Utah where they married and have perfect little kids. Alyse, her husband Dan and the others have become true Texans ya'll, and can use the word ya'll three times in one sentence, ya'll. The Midlanders tend to be extremely friendly and gracious because that is about all they can offer ya'll visitors.

We've been making this trip for some 25-odd years, and to make the trip more interesting, we chose to approach the city from a different direction each time. I remember coming up from San Antonio, when the road was full of testosterone-driven tarantulas trying to find the females who live in holes, preferably alone. I'd live alone too, if my only choice was ugly and hairy, and had nine eyes. For miles down the road we could see these arachnid monsters creeping across, seeking a female whose holes were definitely not in the blacktop. If anything had happened to the car, I was determined to stay locked inside until help came, or until I died from fear. Can spiders crawl up the wheel wells?

The year Texas was in a cold snap, we had a thermometer in our car and wondered how low it would register. We watched with interest as the temperature reached 0, then minus 1 and clear down to minus 10 degrees as we slid through Amarillo and headed south. When we got to Midland, the Weidmann's grass was covered with ice.

One year we drove down to spend Christmas, and went through Gallop, New Mexico. We were engulfed in a sea of pickup trucks loaded high with multiple bikes and tires, and other stuff tucked in between, all headed south. When we stopped at the motel, we found out that the trucks were headed to Mexico for the holidays, a sort of Feliz Navidad for our southern neighbors from their relatives in the USA.

We drove through Roswell, New Mexico taking a couple of our grand kids home after a summer visit in Highland. Those townspeople take full advantage of their brush with the aliens, and have opened an interesting International UFO Museum and Research Center. The kids and I made aluminum foil hats so the aliens couldn't steal our brains, and bought tickets to go into the museum. Bob was so embarrassed that he just sat in the car. The way he keeps forgetting things, I think the aliens might have stolen some of his brain because he refused to wear an aluminum foil hat for protection.

The last time we drove to Midland about three years ago, a road weary old Bob said, "If I ever suggest we drive this instead of flying, please hit me up side the head with a board!" Not feeling up to clobbering my husband with a board, we have flown down to see the family ever since. Thanksgiving, here we come and we'll be ever so thankful when we get there!

TOO GOOD TO BE TRUE

We had a nice visit with our old friends Mona and Harold last week. Harold and Bob were professors at Southern Utah University, and the four of us were next door neighbors for more years than we care to admit. After our kids had flown the coop, we liked to travel together, and we had some great times.

One summer, a travel agency in Texas advertised a $39 round trip air fare to Hawaii, if they could plan and book our trip. Well, we weren't stupid, no siree! We were from Cedar City, Utah for goodness sake, so we called the Better Business Bureau in Texas to check on this company. We found that they were legit and had no complaints against them, so in March we signed up and sent our money.

We didn't hear anything for a month, so we called Texas and found that they had transferred our contract to a travel company in Chicago. *Oh great,* we thought. *Now our tickets are in the hands of the mafia.* We called Chicago and were relieved to hear that they were working on a lovely four island jaunt for us, and our $39 air fare was still good.

But we waited, and we waited, and by May when we hadn't heard anything, we began to worry in earnest. We started making phone calls every day. We talked to agents, assistant supervisors and supervisors, and when we demanded to talk to the CEO, they put us on hold for an hour until we hung up in desperation. We were thinking that we had been taken in; that it *was* too good to be true.

Finally it came down to the last week before we were scheduled to leave. Bob and Harold were calling twice a day, and not being very polite about it either. I think we mentioned something about sending out a hit man to shoot them in their knees. Someone in Chicago finally got the hint that we really wanted that trip, and realized the tickets wouldn't reach us in time unless they sent them Federal Express. Well now, Cedar City doesn't have a FE office. Did they think we were a big city or something? So they promised we could pick them up in St. George on Friday and that was the day we were due to fly out of Las Vegas.

We were frantic, and while Harold and Bob attended to their graduation duties, I was assigned to stay by the phone waiting for St. George to let us know if our tickets had arrived. When the call came, I was so excited I drove down to school, sneaked down the graduation line to the faculty and knocked on Bob's mortarboard to let him know we were good to go!

Within three hours we packed up Harold's van, picked up our tickets in St. George, and made the drive to the Las Vegas airport. We left the van in a fenced area close to the airport, and they shuttled us in to catch our $39 flight. We heaved a collective sign of relief on the plane, and we snoozed all the way to Hawaii.

It was gorgeous! In spite of all the worry and stress, our accommodations were wonderful. They were big two bedroom condos with living rooms and full kitchens, and except for our car from Rent-a-Wreck, we were top drawer small town folks.

Since Mona and I were on a *no cooking* vacation, we only used the kitchens to pour milk on our cereal for breakfast, and the rest of the time we dined out. On Maui, we saw an advertisement for Fast Freddie's Authentic Hawaiian Food. Although we didn't think Freddy was a Hawaiian name, off we went to find his authentic food. It was a split level building with a store on top and Freddy's place down stairs. We walked in, and Mona and I took one look and tried to make a run back out the door, but our husbands caught us, and said, "At least let's give it a try now we're here." It was scary! None of the chairs matched, the tables were wooden platforms, and the only people in the place were a couple of women making leis in the corner, and a few barefoot kids running around the tables. One of the ladies told us to sit and then yelled to someone in the back to come help us. Mona and I tried to keep our eyes off the grime and grease on the walls, but the menus weren't much cleaner either. We ordered a Hawaiian salad with mango dressing and coconut mahi-mahi. What a surprise...it was wonderful! We just closed our eyes and enjoyed every bite.

The next day, the men said we could choose the place to eat, and Mona and I picked the best looking Chinese restaurant in town. It had a fountain in front, with lovely oriental ambiance overlooking waterfalls streaming down the mountains outside. But the food was just awful! They even managed to mess up the rice. It was hard and crunchy. Where's a McDonald's when you need one?

We loved Hawaii, and the flight home came too soon. We landed in Las Vegas at eleven thirty at night and called the car place to pick us up only to find that it had closed at eleven, and wouldn't be open again until seven a.m. Picture four weary travelers; each with a large suitcase, a small carry on, four cases of authentic Hawaiian pineapples, and two bags of sweet Maui onions. We knew we couldn't all fit in one cab. We couldn't shove all of our goodies in one of those tiny airport lockers, and Mona and I weren't about to leave our pineapples and onions. Our only option was to hunker down at the airport until morning. Bob and Harold each found a bench and were soon snoring away, but it was a little harder for Mona and I who are used to a pillow, a blanket and some privacy.

First we tried shopping, but the stores were closing and they hustled us out the doors so they could lock up. We cleaned out our purses and repacked our suitcases. That took up an hour or so. Then we found where they parked the people mover carts. We hoped that someone had left a key in the ignition, and we could race up and down the isles. We got the giggles over that picture and the night guard became suspicious and asked us to back away from the carts. By this time we were feeling a little silly and wondered if the guard would like to pat us down to see if we were carrying concealed weapons. We'd have been glad to pay him for the excitement. Weapons! If we could find a knife we could cut open one of our precious pineapples. Maybe not. That would make a big mess and we'd have to clean it up. From then on things got a little hazy, but we didn't end up in the office of the National Security Administration, so that was good.

Finally morning came, and we woke up the men, collected our luggage, and retrieved the van. Mona and I draped ourselves over the luggage and the boxes of pineapples, and had a richly deserved three hour nap all the way home to our city, arriving just in time to make a lovely pineapple fruit salad for lunch.

DANGLING FROM A PARACHUTE

You might wonder why a 75 year old great grandmother would allow herself to be towed over the water by a Mexican driving an old beat up boat, while dangling precariously from a parachute. Probably because she was full of tequila. Oh, wait...I can't use that excuse because I don't drink anything stronger than Pepsi on the rocks.

Well, it all started out innocently enough, when Karen called to invite us to join her and Bobby on a Mexican Riviera cruise in celebration of their 30th wedding anniversary. My Bob and I are always ready for a trip. Our suitcases and passports are stored by the back door in case of (1. an invitation to go somewhere (2. a tsunami hits Draper (3. the space shuttle needs our help in outer space, or which ever one comes first. So (1. we grabbed our bags and met the Weidmanns in San Pedro and we were off again.

I love cruises. We get up late and can have eggs Benedict for breakfast every morning. They're my personal favorite. If we're in port, I do a little shopping. I like to bargain, especially if it's stuff I don't really need, which pretty much includes everything. As Bob likes to remind me, "At your age you don't need anymore *stuff*."

Afterward we hurry back to the ship for a leisurely lunch and then it's off to the room for a nice nap. Karen wakes us up in time for our dancing lessons, or craft classes, or art auction. There's plenty to do on board. We have early dinner reservations, so we clean up and get ready to dine at 5:30. They serve exotic five-course meals, and nowadays for an exotic price you can buy the chef's cookbook.   I didn't buy one though, because they would not let me bargain for a lower price, and Bob would not let me cook with wine and garlic anyway.

They have a big production show every night in the theater. It's fun, but a little on the loud side, so Bob and I sit there with tissues in our ringing ears. After the show, guests are free to gamble, drink, and disco, but since we don't like any of those options, we just waddle around the promenade deck a few times and it's off to read before bedtime. Cruise ships have wonderful libraries. We spend a lot of time there, reading, playing games, or drawing.

When we got to Mazatlan, Weidmanns had arranged to go parasailing from a beach that had a brisk wind about the speed of a small hurricane. Bob and I went to cheer them on. We waited in the sun on that beach, for a couple of hours watching people take off and land, without even getting their feet wet. Bobby even kept his hat and sun glasses on as he went up. Karen did a lot of giggling, and said that ten minutes in the air was too short a time. So, taking courage, I walked right up to the man in charge and said, "Yo quiera birdo," which means "I wish to go flying," I think. Bob gave him $30 and he called over two husky guys to help me. They put a life vest on me, and strapped me into a fancy straight jacket harness. In their best English, which was better than my Spanish, they said when the leader on the beach waves a green flag at me, I was to pull down hard on the right strap of the parachute, and I would float gently down to the beach. They even tied a pink ribbon on the right strap, so I wouldn't make a mistake and land in the water.

The boat took off just as they yelled at me to sit back into the harness...too late. I made the whole trip with one leg hanging lopsided in the harness. Other than that, I quite enjoyed myself up there looking down at Mazatlan and the bay, until I saw some crazy guy waving a green flag. Oh, wait! That's *my* crazy guy, and I reached for the strap with the pink ribbon and pulled as hard as I could. The parachute came down slowly over the heads of three frantic Mexicans and one worried husband, and I settled gently on the beach without even jarring my sore knees. All in all, it was an exhilarating experience and yes, I *would* do it again some time. But next time I'm in Mexico, it's the zip line through the jungle for this old lady!

YOU TARZAN, ME JEAN

Our latest adventure was zip lining through the jungle treetops in Puerto Vallarta...Bob, Tarzan, me Jane, or in this case, Jean. How did this happen to a nice old retired couple like us, you ask? Karen and Bobby tried this adventure in October and decided it would be the very thing to put a little zip in our cruising, so she made reservations for us. I'm not sure it was kindness on her part, or if she was trying to get an early inheritance, but when we got to port there was a bus was waiting, and off we went. We bounced through town on a cobblestone road, bumped onto a blacktop road peppered with pot holes the size of moon craters, and lastly swayed onto a dirt road with one lane only. At the end of the road and half way up the mountain, there was a small cantina and a petting zoo that consisted of tarantulas, a boa constrictor, iguanas, and assorted monkeys. For a small fee we were welcome to have any of these indigenous creepy crawlers climb up our arms and rest on our heads. We declined that opportunity. We're old, not crazy!

We were greeted enthusiastically by six young, muscled hombres, who were to be our guides through the trees. They fitted us each with a harness that resembled thong underwear with suspenders, and tightened it firmly between our legs. A hard hat and a pulley with handle bars, completed our ensemble. They sat us down in a little thatch hut, and our amigos explained how everything worked, and we were not to worry. Then off we went...trudging farther up the mountain. That was when my asthma decided to kick in, and I was panting so hard Tarzan took pity on me and hauled my pulley and me up to the first tree. The tree had a spiral staircase up to a platform, where one at a time we were hooked to wire cable. When we got to the platform Tarzan decided I should go first so he could keep an eye on me, so

Juan lifted me up by my harness and attached me to the cable, and there I hung, looking down into a chasm filled with green stuff.

"Are you ready to fly?" Juan said.

"No, not yet, " said fearless Jean.

"Ready now?"

"No," said I.

"No comprendo," said Juan, as he pushed me off the platform.

Needless to say, I arrived safely on the other side, and discovered I was not going to die after all. Besides, sliding was much easier than climbing, so I was a happy little flier.

There were about ten lines of various lengths and and altitudes. One of the longest was a hundred feet and over a river, and I'm sure I could see alligators smiling up at me smacking their chops. However, they would not eat me alive, because the fall would probably kill me, except for my head which was held in place by a hard hat. That darn thing kept sliding down over my eyes.

The last span had dual cables so two people could race down side by side. I won the race, probably because Juan pushed me early and Tarzan waited until they said "go."

When we got to the bottom at the cantina, we realized that we were by far the oldest fliers that day, and they made a big fuss over us and treated us to a free Coke.

What's next? We'll see what Karen has in store for us. She really does love us, you know.

CROSSING THE BORDER

It seems like any one can cross our southern border into USA now days, even suspected terrorists.   But crossing our northern border from Canada became a real challenge for a bus load of us senior citizens. Before 9-11 we could traipse back and forth into Canada with just our driver licenses, but those days apparently are gone for good. Take our recent experience...please.

To catch our cruise ship to Alaska, Bob and I flew into Seattle, and then were taken by bus to Vancouver, Canada where our ship was docked. There is a simple explanation for this; air fare is cheaper into the USA than into Canada, and my dear Bob is very careful with his money thus allowing for more cruises. When crossing into Canada by bus, all we had to do was stay in our seats and hold our open passports up by our wrinkled faces to be sure we matched the picture, although since they put a stamp across the picture we looked like Scarface characters.

After a lovely cruise in Alaska, we prepared to come back home. We were all given colored tags for our luggage and were supposed to leave the ship with the group of the same color. Ours were chocolate brown. When we got off the ship and cleared customs, we found ourselves in a long line of people waiting for a bus...to the Vancouver airport! This was *not* our destination. We needed the bus for Seattle, and all of the people in line had black tags, not brown. One nervous little lady in a red coat rushed off to consult with another lady in a red coat with a clip board. They both hustled back, took us and our luggage out of line, and sat us in chairs next to the door while they debated what to do. After much talking and gesturing they directed us down to the parking lot on the lower level that I hoped wasn't in hell. When we got there they told us to board the bus quickly as another bus needed that parking spot immediately. I think we were getting the bum's rush.

We hurried on the bus and were off to Seattle. The time was good. The trip to Seatac airport took about four hours and our flight didn't leave until 4:15. The real problem came as we reached the border. There were long lines of cars, trucks, and buses streaming into the USA. The car and truck lanes were moving right along, but the buses were at a standstill. After 20 minutes our bus moved to the corner where there was a round driveway and five buses in front of us. As we watched, a bus pulled up to the side of the building, everyone got off, took their luggage out from underneath the bus and disappeared inside the building. Then one by one they came out the other side, looking very disgruntled. Slowly they climbed onto their bus again and were finally allowed to enter the good old USA. My imagination went wild. The average age of these passengers must have been all of 70 years old. Were they being strip-searched? How many explosives can an old duffer hide in his belly wrinkles?

Our bus driver warned us to keep our complaints to ourselves as the border guards can tie up a bus for hours if they get mad. When the guard finally came over to us, the driver told him we were all American citizens, had been through customs, and the bus cargo had been sealed as we left the ship. He turned with a "humpf," and walked into that ominous building. So we sat, and we sat, and I felt Bob getting angrier by the minute. His ears turned a lovely shade of pink. I tried to start a sing-a-long, but it ended up as a solo rendition of "My Bonnie Lies Over the Ocean," and frankly my voice is not that good.   Finally I just shut up and and sat quietly working my Sudoku puzzles.

After sitting in the same spot for an hour watching the trucks and cars stream past us, another guard came out to ask where we were going. The bus driver told him where we had been and where we were going, and he said,"Well go then. What are you waiting around here for?" He didn't have to tell us twice. The bus driver about dumped us all on the floor getting out of there and across the border.

We made it to the airport just in time to drag our luggage up a hill, check in and get right on our plane. I think crossing the border would be so much easier if all the good guys just wore a gold star on their foreheads like we did in Sunday School when we were little. As for me, I'm never leaving the United States again, at least until our next cruise.

CALIFORNIA, HERE WE COME

Did someone say Bob and I were getting too old to withstand the "slings and arrows of outrageous" road trips? We are nothing of the sort. Take last winter for instance. Growing tired of the snow and cold, we started out for the Weidmann condo in Palm Desert, California for a little stay in the sun. As we left home the sky was gray with light snow falling. We had driven in the snow all that winter, so no big deal. But as we got to Cove Fort and were passing an oil tanker, we hit a patch of black ice. Bob had the choice of smacking into the back of the tanker or slipping down a seven foot gully. He chose the gully. He was masterful; steering right between two metal mile markers and right down to the bottom, while keeping the car upright. Now any self-respecting passenger would have her life flashing before her eyes, but my selfish thought was, "I'm glad we're in Bob's car and not my cool Lincoln."

When the car came to a stop we just sat there. We didn't know whether to laugh or cry, so we settled for, "Wow, what an trip!" Finally Bob pushed his door open scratching the corner, and surveyed his poor car. Besides the door scratches, the outside mirror on his side was broken off, but me and my side were undamaged, except for my confidence in driving in the snow.

As Bob was taking some pictures, a policeman stopped on the road above us to help. "Are you all right?" he called to us.

"Yes," answered Bob, "but I thought we were going to die!"

"I'm glad you didn't. Then I would have to do a lot more paper work." He called a tow truck from Cove Fort and waited until it arrived. It only took five minutes. The tow truck guy said, "You did some tricky driving. I pulled a car out of here last week that rolled twice." When he got us hitched up like a fish on a line, the car began to fishtail back and forth, so the tow truck driver got out his shovel and dug down to the dirt where there was some traction. He got us up to the road and took off his hook. Miracles of miracles, our car drove right down the road without even a wobble.

By the time we got to Cove Fort, I had my shoes and coat on so I could go to the bathroom and make sure I had not went my pants. Meanwhile the tow guy was showing Bob how worn our tires were and offering him the deal of a life time on four new tires...with the tow thrown in for free. Bob, not fresh off the farm, called Big O in Salt Lake to check the price on their tires, and decided that we would accept the tow guy's offer. An hour later we headed back down the road with new tires, dented door, and a heart full of thankfulness.

After a stay in Mesquite, we got to Palm Desert about four p.m. the next day, just in time for another adventure. Old folks like us don't need GPS...we have Map Quest, and it never lies. Wrong! It brought us right up to the back gate of the compound where the condo was located. There was a big sign; "Do not enter...or a monster will rise up out of the road and eat your brand new tires. Use the front gate!" Where in the heck was the front gate? Brigham Young didn't make it down as far as Palm Desert to lay out the streets in nice neat squares. To make matters worse, we couldn't remember the name of the condo complex. Talk about your senior moments. We made a frantic call to Bobby in Texas and he told us the name of the place and the street where it was located. And lo and behold, that was the street we were calling from, so we drove west for a few miles, and there it was. We were saved again!

We stayed for a week, but saw very little sun. In fact the rain got so bad they were inviting people to pick up sand bags at their nearest fire station. We decided to leave for home while we could still get out without an ark. And therein lies another tale.

WHERE'S MY ARK?

In our recent trip to southern California, it rained buckets. It was the worst storm in that area in 50 years. In Utah we measure our rain in tenths of an inch, and at Palm Desert it had rained three to four inches a day, with more rain predicted for the end of the week. Bob and I had been there for almost a week and were starting to get moldy, so we decided we had better get out of town while we could. When there was a little break on Thursday morning we left, taking the southern route through Blythe because there was five feet of snow over Cajon Pass and cars needed chains. From the time we left the house there was fog and rain. Bob said, "Are you nervous?"

"Nah," sez I, lying through my teeth.

"Then take your blanket off your head and help me keep an eye on the road, will you?" Being an obedient wife, I did as I was told, but I was hoping he wouldn't ask me to strap a flashlight to my head, and stand up through the sun roof like a beacon.

At Blythe, we turned on to Highway 95, a two lane goat trail, and the storm hit in earnest. Every low place in the road had its own flowing river, carrying rocks and debris along the desert floor. Mostly they were small rivers, but they kept getting bigger and bigger until I expected to see Noah come floating down, gathering up coyotes and lizards.

Then we came to the raging mother of all rivers. It was sending plumes of water against the rocks, spraying four feet high. Even the big trucks and trailers didn't dare cross. So there were a line of vehicles on both sides of the river. We got out and took pictures and got soaked. When we climbed back in the car we decided to turn around and go back to Blythe. We drove back

112

down the road two miles only to find that stream we'd forded an hour ago was now a roaring river, with a line of cars waiting to cross.

So back we went to the *desert Mississippi* for another wait, and in about an hour the water subsided enough to cross. We drove on into Needles. But by then the rain was coming down so hard that our wipers were swishing in frantic mode. We would have pulled off to the side of the road, but the sides had all been washed away. We made it to the Needles city limits, just as the police came in behind us and closed off the road. We chose the cleanest looking motel, grabbed a burger and a salad at McDonald's, and crashed (in bed that is).

The next morning the rains held off until we turned onto Highway 95, but they were light this time. The road had dried out, leaving potholes the size of hot tubs. I swear I saw lizards in their speedos skittering from one pot hole to another.

When we got to Henderson it was smooth sailing, except for a snow flurry or two, so we kept going until we got home to good old Draper. It was quite a wet adventure. Bob said we can always stay at home safe and warm, but we wouldn't get to go anywhere. So we packed a tent, umbrellas and fishing gear in our trunk, and we're ready to go again!

DISCOVERING THE ERIE CANAL

Yes, I know you're thinking that's already been done, but not by these two old codgers together with Cap'n Bobby, first mate Karen, and Gilligan aka Brett. And there's nothing like a leisurely six-mile an hour cruise down a peaceful canal to help you discover the flow of life.

Bob was looking for cruises on the computer when he found the Mid-Lakes Navigation Company, where for a mere $2975 you can captain your own Lock Master Canal boat for a week-long vacation on the Erie Canal. For a brief moment I envisioned myself chained to the business end of an oar, while Bob pounded out a cadence on a water barrel. But when the pamphlet came it showed a comfortable 41 foot craft, with two bedrooms, two baths, a shower, stove, refrigerator and dinette, and all with "the solid feel of the brass and mahogany tiller for precise control and graceful maneuvering." Sounded great. Where do we sign up?

Then realization hit us that we might, just might, be too old to do this alone. So we called on our co-conspirators Karen and Bobby, and sure enough...they were ready for a new adventure. Karen is our computer guru, and arranged for us all to meet at a nice hotel in Rochester the night before we sailed. They also brought along their 16 year old Brett, and he proved to be worth his weight, which is considerable, in gold.

The next morning we took a cab to the grocery store and then on to Macedon, New York. There she was...our beautiful chocolate brown and mint green *Cayuga*, ready and waiting for us. She was spotless, filled with water and fuel, dishes and cookware, sheets, blankets, towels, and with three bicycles tied on top. All we had to do was climb aboard with our luggage and our food.

Eric, from the company, came on board and appointed Bobby Cap'n. Being a curious lot, we all stood around learned what to do, as Bobby pulled away from the dock and started down the canal. Steering a 41 foot barge with a rudder is like maneuvering a speed boat with a ping pong paddle. There is a forward and reverse, and side thrusters which the Cap'n liked to use, because they were noisy and made us all jump. There are not many hazards on the 300 mile canal, except for the low bridges, mooching ducks and geese, and the 30 plus locks that raised or lowered our barge. So Eric had us sail to the first lock. Karen went on the radio and said, "This is the *Cayuga,* heading east...will you please open the lock?" The lockmaster answered back, "Aye, *Cayuga*. The gate is open and waiting."

We sailed into the lock against the cement wall, where there were ropes to hold. Karen grabbed the rope from the stern, and Brett got the rope on the bow. The gate closed behind us and the water level started down. Our rope holders slid their gloved hands down the slimy ropes as we descended 26 feet. The lockmaster stood at the end of the lock and visited with us until we were at the bottom. He then opened the outer gates and we sailed through, just like the big guys. Eric had the Cap'n turn us around and go back through the lock the other direction, and we went back up. The last instructions from Eric were on backing the boat into the dock. He jumped off, gave us his emergency phone number, and bid us bon voyage. On the next lock I thought it might be fun for Brett to hang on the top of the rope while it dropped the boat down and then he could slide down the rope to the boat again. His mother voted *no*, and threatened to keel haul me if I suggested it again.

Navigation is easy on this canal that only runs east and west, so we headed off into the sunset toward Niagara Falls. The next hazard was a lift bridge that came up soon after we were turned loose by Eric. Karen called ahead, and the bridge master acknowledged, stopped the car traffic, and raised the bridge so we could sail under it. The next bridge was about a half mile away and run by the same bridge master. He lowered the bridge behind us, ran down the stairs, jumped in his car and drove over to the next bridge, raised it up, and let us sail underneath. The lock masters and bridge masters were accommodating, even taking us to the grocery store in their cars when it was too far for the bikes. There are beautiful little villages all along the canal and most of them had docking facilities with electricity and water for traveling boats. There were not many boats on the canal this early in the season, but there is a good path that runs parallel to the canal. The joggers and bikers on the path wanted to race our boat. We lost.

When we got to Lockport, the closest dock to Niagara Falls, we tied up and called a car rental place. They brought us a car, and off we went to visit the Falls. Brett wanted to sail over the Falls in our boat, but the Company frowns on that sort of thing. We went into Canada and gave the Falls our Oooo's and Ahhhh's. The Weidmanns did go over the Falls, but inside a helicopter, and then it was back to our sweet *Cayuga* for bed.

After being accosted by ducks and geese for bread scraps, we turned around and headed east on the canal. We stopped along the way and ate white hots, (a delicious white meat hot dog that tastes like sausage), Greek pitas, New York pizza, and frozen custard. Those things didn't help my diet, but I enjoyed them thoroughly.

After a week of exploring the canal we reluctantly took our *Cayuga* back to its real owners, and said goodbye. We had a day to spend visiting some of the LDS Church sites in Palmyra, so we rented another car, piled in and we were off again. They were well preserved and peaceful, and put a nice finish to our trip.

This must be the time of canals for us...last year, the Panama Canal, this year, the Erie Canal, next year, maybe the Suez Canal, but only if the government in Egypt can get it's act together.

Hawai'i...Perfect Mission for Seniors

Serving a mission made us feel useful, and kept us from meddling in our kids' lives for a while.

MISSION MELTDOWN

Bob and I were delighted when our mission call came to Kailua Kona, Hawaii as Church Education Service missionaries. We had visited there several times and even spent an entire week before going on to Australia in 1985. It is one of the few places left in the islands that resembles an old fishing village. We loved it then and we love it now.

But as a missionary, I was ill prepared for the humidity as I stepped off that airplane in July. We left Salt Lake at four a.m., flew to San Francisco and onto a flight to Kona. The Kona airport has an early 1940 motif, with thatch roofs and a portable stairway from plane to tarmac. When I walked down the steps at high noon, I was dressed like a proper missionary. I had well coiffed red hair (my favorite wig) and impeccable makeup, complete with blemish cover, base, blush, eye brows, eye shadow, mascara, and lips carefully outlined and filled in with a modest peach color. I was wearing a sea green suit with a jacket, slip, panty hose, and sensible pumps...with enclosed heels and toes. As I walked confidently into the future I was hit by an 89 degree wall of heat, with 110% humidity. I walked to the grass hut to pick up my 150 pounds of luggage and books, and I had begun to melt. Perspiration was making little rivulets of makeup down my face that dripped off my chin and soaked down into my cleavage. The front and back of my shirt were stuck to my body and by the time I got my jacket off, Elder Honey (Bob) took one look at me and said, "Oh, you poor thing!" But he didn't offer to help with my luggage. He was trying to cope with his own. President Bauer of Hilo met us and hung a beautiful, but heavy shell lei around my neck, which promptly slid off and ended down around my elbows, pinning them to my sweaty body.

When we arrived at our land lady's house where we were to rent rooms, I was soaked through. I slogged in with my luggage and made wheel marks all across her white carpet. Before we could sit down or change clothes, I was cleaning carpet. I had hoped to unpack, and put on something better suited for paradise, but no luck. The dear lady had fixed us a sandwich and a glass of water. She didn't have potato chips or soda pop because they were not healthy. We did get her hooked on some of those evil foods like cake and cookies before we came back home, but not that day.

Good...nap time I thought, since we had been up since three a.m. But no, again. We had to go pick up our leased car. I did manage to change my into a dress and ditch the wig. I was much cooler when President Bauer took us to see the Church and the Temple in Kona. Then off to Ke'ei 45 minutes to the south and to Honoka which was 90 minutes to the north to visit the LDS Church buildings there. Hawaii, or the Big Island, is exactly that; a *big* island. All of the other island could fit in the big island twice. But the delicious delight of the day was a little shop in Honoka that sold malasadas. That is a large square Portuguese sugar doughnut with gooey cream in the center. Along with fresh pineapple and macadamia nuts, malasadas are on my favorite food list.

We finally got back to our island home about nine p.m. (or two a.m. Utah time) so tired that we could barely flop into bed. The next morning I went right out and bought a couple of muu muus and a pair of flip flops, and I went native for the rest of our mission.

MANGO WARS

There was a mango tree in our back yard in Hawaii that grew big, three-pound mangoes. They were beautiful, juicy and delicious. The problem was that if they weren't picked up as soon as they fell, a weaselly little varmint called a mongoose would sneak in and nibble until there was nothing left for us. Mongooses were brought to the islands in the 1800's to keep the rat population under control. The problem was, the rats were night critters and the mongooses liked the daylight, and so they changed their diet from carnivores to omnivores, and ate whatever came across their path.

Most Hawaiians considered them as pests. However, we knew one family who actually kept a mongoose as a pet, much to the dismay of their neighbors. It stole their fruit and killed their chickens. It was a cute little thing, but when it got nervous, it wet on whoever was holding it, and that seemed to be everyone except their family. Its name was Sparkle. It should have been Sprinkle.

Anyhow, back to my story...Bob had decided that those mangoes in the back yard were *his,* and he didn't intend to share with some stray opportunist weasel. So the first thing every morning, he hurried out and gathered up *his* mangoes. He didn't do too well at first and the score was: mongoose-4, human-2, and Bob was not happy. Something had to change. He threatened to trap the little pest and haul it up to Waimea and let it loose to eat their mangoes, but he couldn't locate a live trap and we really didn't want to kill it.

It came down to the last two mangoes of the season. Bob decided to tie plastic bags on the tree so the fruit would fall into the bags and out of reach for the thieving mongoose. But when

122

he came back out of the door with the bags, one of the mangoes was on the ground with a juice stained mongoose hovering over it. Bob was furious! He ran at his enemy, whistling as loud as he could and whirling the plastic bags through the air. The poor little mongoose took one look at that crazy man, and ran like the devil, over the top of the fence and into the ravine below. Bob grabbed the last mango off the tree, and the chewed fruit on the ground and stormed into the house. Aha! Elder Honey had won.

A half an hour later I saw a disgruntled mongoose come up on the porch and peer in the glass door, undoubtedly looking for the rest of *his* mango. He couldn't find it, so he walked away in a snit. Well, that might have been the end of the mango wars, but the bananas were getting ripe.

I was telling one of our Hawaiian students about our mongoose adventures, and that I thought they were cute little fellars, and he said, "Ya...and they taste good too. Kinda like chicken."

LEARNING MOORE HAWAIIAN

While we lived in Kona for a year I wanted to learn all I could about the people and the language.   Hawaiian is mostly a dead language, but with its last gasp many natives are trying hard to hold on, and there is a renewed interest in learning it in the schools. They've always given you an enthusiastic "aloha" at the beginning of their meetings, and "aloha" as you leave. That's an all purpose word that means hello, goodbye, love, and why don't you haoles (non-natives) just send your money over here and quit messing up our beaches?

Unlike some languages that roll their r's or make guttural growls in the throat, Hawaiians pride themselves on how many vowels they can string together in a word. They tell you the language is simple...you just say every letter. Simple for them, but not simple for an old haole, like me. For example, take Keauhou, the name of a bay just south of Kona where we practiced our ukuleles. You think it would be five syllables, Ke-a-u-ho-u, right? Wrong! The natives say Kee-a-hou in just three syllables.

The Hawaiians are very patient and anxious to help you learn, but on the other hand they love to laugh when your pronunciation is a little off...or a lot off, as the case may be. One of our students was a beautiful young lady in Waimea (two syllables) whose name is Heuaheamoanianilehuaokkumupika (twelve syllables). She goes by the name Moani, but her name means "when the soft winds blow down into the green valley, I'll be coming home to dance the hula with you under the moon," or something like that. Many Hawaiian names mean something wonderful like Kapono (righteous) or Lanakila (victorious), and they love their names. Another of our students named Carl, prefers his Hawaiian name, Kaiwi (three syllables).

I love the islands and read all the history I could find. I learned that the State Motto is: *Perpetuated is the life of the land by its righteousness.* Sounds like something right out of the scriptures. Moani told me that every school keiki can recite the motto in Hawaiian: *Ua mau ke eea a ka aine I ka pono.* I wanted to use the motto in my talks I gave at church, so I tried it out on Moani in my best Hawaiian. She burst out laughing. I said, "If I say that in church everyone is going to laugh right out loud, aren't they?"

"Yes, pretty much," she said, wiping the tears from her eyes. Soon after that she was called on a mission to Japan, so she didn't get to laugh at me when we spoke in the Waimea Ward.

Hawai'ians have another little trick they like to use. They add an apostrophe here and there. They stick it the words so you have a chance to catch a breath, and get ready for the next set of vowels coming up. There's Honoka'a, Na'alehu, and the ever popular 'Akaka Falls. Even the name Hawaii is correctly spelled Hawai'i.

Then, just when you think you're getting pretty good with those words, they hit you with a little pidgin: "Howzit Braddah and Sisah! Bimeby we go Ho'olaule's widdah kane and wahine and choke ono humuhumu nukunuku a pua'a? E komo mai. Mahalo." You gotta love 'em, even if you can't always understand 'em! And we do love them! Aloha.

SPAM JAM

Hawaiians love Spam. They even have a special holiday to celebrate the canned goody called *Spam Jam*. I first noticed the island's love affair with Spam when I had breakfast in Honolulu, at McDonald's, of all places. I ordered the scrambled egg platter that came with toast, hash browns and this unfamiliar slice of meat. "What is this?" I asked Bob, as I waved a forkful under his nose. He sniffed, but did not bite the bait and pronounced it to be Spam. "How do you know?" I said.

"Because it says so on the menu...Spam and eggs," he disdainfully pointed out. Well, duh!

Spam, do they still eat that stuff? I thought victory in WW II meant freedom from having to eat Spam, and after trying to serve it to my college roomies, I had forgotten it was a food choice. I was wrong, and in fact, Hawaiians consume more Spam per capita than any other state in the Union.

Before I belittle a regional treat I decided to find out more about the stuff, and so I Googled Spam, the meat. It was first produced in 1937. It's almost as old as me, but much better preserved. It was named by contest for spiced ham...Spam. Over six billion cans have been sold, and that's enough to fill every tummy in China and any other developing country that is in need. There is also an official Spam museum in Austin, Minnesota. That is also the designated Spam city, and home of a mascot named Spammy the Pig. I remember an episode of *MASH*, when they molded Spam into the shape of a lamb for Easter...a Spam lamb.

Since making these startling revelations, I've noticed that Spam turns up at every ward dinner and buffet we've attended in the islands. One of our sweet seminary teachers made us a special breakfast of egg casserole with a Spam garnish on top. Jokingly, I asked, "Do I get Spam and poi? I love fresh poi."

But seriously, Spam is a whole different humuhumu nukunuku a pua'a in the world of ono pupu. The grocery stores frequently have specials on cans of Spam, $1.99 a can or $3.98 to buy a can and get one free. On *Spam Jam* day, the local holiday, they offered Spamburgers, fried Spam, baked Spam, cream of Spam soup, Spam stew, tempura Spam, chopped Spam spread, Spam and pineapple stir fry, and chocolate coated Spam. Okay, I made up that last one up.

I developed a whole new reverence for Spam, until I read the ingredients on the label. There are 180 calories per slice, 140 grams of fat, and 790 mg of sodium. Hormel, ever conscious of our health has now given us choices; regular Spam, Spam Lite, Low Sodium Spam, and Spicy Spam. They have entire rows of Spam in the grocery stores in Hawaii.

But is all that stuff good for my little 75 year old body? I think I'd better stick to baked humuhumu nukunuku a pua'a which incidentally is the official State Fish of Hawaii. Please, my Hawaiian friends, I mean no disrespect, so don't make me a persona non grata. I love pineapple and macadamia nuts.

But all this talk of meat has made me hungry. I think I'll lengthen my shuffle to the kitchen and have a Spamwich...lite, that is.

TEENIE JEANNIE, GUTTER BALL QUEENIE

While in Hawaii, the students in our church class had been asking us to go bowling with them and the young elders who were serving LDS missions. Apparently there was a question of who were the best...the kanes (men) or wahines (women). I kept finding excuses, as I am the single worst bowler on the entire island or any island for that matter. That's not humility, that's a fact. So when we arrived at the bowling alley there were about ten kids from our classes, six young men, and some little brothers and sisters that came with their baby sitters.

Bob put a pair of too large, clown shoes on my feet (they didn't have shoes my size), stuck a bright orange ball on my fingers, and led me up to the alley. And there I stood, with *klutz* written on my forehead. My first ten balls were all gutter balls, while all around me there were strikes and spares, followed by high fives. I watched in amazement as three of the elders palmed the balls, not using the finger holes, then slammed them down the alley knocking the pins down right and left! It was amazing. I could tell they had bowled before.

The scores were magically recorded on an electronic scoreboard in the sky, and there for all the world to see was *JAM 000*. I was mortified!

But then I began to get the sympathy treatment. One of the young ladies told me to point my thumb right at the pins as I released the ball. How could I do that when my thumb was stuck in a hole inside my bowling ball?

Bob told me not to try any fancy foot work. "Just walk up to the alley and gently release the ball." I did as he suggested, and my ball went down the alley so slowly that the pin setter was picking up the pins by the time it got to the end. It rumbled harmlessly under the pins.

Next, Bob brought over a little rack that the kids use to direct their balls. I put the ball at the top and it just rolled down the alley. It did hit the pins, but it was going so slowly my score was in the 2s or 3s. Big deal!

Elder Rice decided I needed some divine intervention. He stood behind me and as I released my ball, he fired a ball right behind it. By the time mine rolled into the gutter, his whizzed by and knocked down all the pins. That worked well, and I was actually scoring. It didn't take me long to figure out I could pad my score by letting the elders bowl with me. Why, I even made a spare!

Bob, on the other hand, is a good bowler. He started out with a couple of spares, and by the end of the games it was just strike, strike, strike! In this case older really is better and he is two years older than me. By the time I get his age I'll be a pro. Until then my title of *Teenie Jeannie, Gutter Ball Queenie* is secure.

UKULELE AND ME

It's official! I am a *professional* ukulele player. Yes sir, the little ukulele band I joined in Hawaii got paid $200 for playing at the Coconut Grove. Now that's not to say I actually got the money. No, the money went to our band for new sound equipment. We needed it badly after our Thanksgiving performance when the rain shorted out our amps.

How did a nice girl like me ever become a "hopping flea" (uke) *professional* you ask...or not? It all began in my college days, when ukuleles and bear-skin coats were having a comeback. My roomies in #408 all bought ukuleles with our lunch money, and we were cool. I learned to fake my way through three- and-a-half songs, and I figured that was good.

But when we got to Kona, the Keauhou shopping center offered free lessons every Friday morning under their grape arbor. The price was right, but you had to have your own uke, and the cheapies they sold to the tourists were not good enough for a potential *professional* like me. So good old Bob scouted out a music store, bought me a nice ukulele with a case, and I was good to go! Bob was the perfect groupie for our band. He would drive me to class, copy music for us, and when we needed decorations, he cut foliage, and hauled our equipment. What a great companion!

Willie, a non Hawaiian, was our teacher/leader, and attendance in the beginner's class varied from week to week depending on what cruise ships were in town. I was a fast learner and practiced in the car with Bob as we drove 120 miles each week to teach religion classes. The advanced class met in the same place an hour later, and after I learned the basic cords, I began sneaking into that class. There were about 25 people and the average age was 65, I pulled up a chair and played along just like a real person, and began collecting my own set of music. Most of the songs were in Hawaiian, so I became very good at lip-sync. These were great people, who not only shared their music, but also their extra bananas, papayas, avocados, and nuts. I figured it was because poor Willie donated his time and needed some reimbursement. Willie was actually a retired chemical engineer from San Francisco, and just picked up the ukulele five years before. So much for his image as a poor Hawaiian.

Our first performance was at the Kona Coffee Festival. I didn't mention that coffee was not on my list of drinks, but the place smelled wonderful. We played for about one half hour and then turned the stage over to the real professionals.

Then we did the Christmas Parade sitting on a foliage covered truck, strumming and singing out vigorous renditions of Mele Kalikamaka. Bob and Willie picked foliage and nailed it to the truck bed. We were #46 right behind three big cement trucks that blew their air horns during the entire parade route and pretty much drowned us out. There were many members of our church downtown shopping, who called out to me. I waved my ukulele. They said, "We didn't know you sang in Hawaiian." Boy, did I have them fooled.

My only problem playing uke was when I got a growth on my index finger. I clipped off what I thought was a little piece of skin, and the next morning it poked up like a tiny flag pole and continued to grow up. The doctor called it "proud flesh" and burned the thing off, and told me I couldn't play in the band for two weeks. Well, I cheated and used three fingers, while holding my bandaged digit out straight. It worked well for most of the chords and I faked the rest.

I love my ukulele and I miss my band friends but lately Andrea has taken up the hobby. This may be the making of a new band right here stateside...the Utah Ukes!

Health and Beauty

for Seniors

We're no beauties, that's for sure... but we do value our health. We talk about it, we worry about it, we dream about it, and sometimes we can even do something about it.

HEAVENLY CHOCOLATE

I received an email yesterday that once-and-for-all proved chocolate is good for you. It comes from a bean, making it a legume and everyone knows your body needs those. It is full of antioxidants and flavanoids and those little suckers help prevent heart disease, cancer, and aging. Be still my heart, and count my blessings for I am an admitted chocoholic and have been since I was a little. I must have inherited this weakness from my father. We used to play hide-and-seek with chocolate chip cookies. He would bring home a quart of chocolate ice cream, and we would grab a spoon and sit at the kitchen table and eat ice cream and our stash of cookies until everything was gone. Mom would then roll us into bed.

As a teenager, hundreds of years ago, my friends and I frequented Cook's Ice Cream Parlor in Provo, whenever we had the money. I always sat by Carol (now my sister-in-law) because she could never finish her chocolate sundae. Being the good buddy that I was, I finished it for her. She is tall and slim, and I am not.

When I grew up and had a kitchen of my own, I could make all kinds of chocolate stuff. I'd bake brownies and cake and cookies, and finish off the left overs while Bob and the kids were at school. When Christmas came I made hand dipped chocolates with cherry, coconut, or fudge centers. Being a devout cook I paid myself tithing by eating every tenth one. Since I needed to have enough to give away, I made huge batches. I learned to make caramel chocolate pretzels and chocolate popcorn and even chocolate dipped potato chips. Our home was a chocolate heaven.

I liked to hide my chocolate candy bars in my underwear drawer. I always smelled good and it did wonders for my love life.

A few years ago, when all the family came home for Christmas, we had a chocolate contest. Each family could take their best shot, as long as it was chocolate. Our neighbors, Mona and Harold were to do the judging. They said it was a tough choice, but they liked Dave and Jon's Black Forest cake with cherries and whipped cream.

I think being brought up on all this chocolate has had a good effect on our children. Karen always asks for power tools and chocolates for Mother's Day. David makes the best chocolate chip and chocolate chocolate chip cookies in Utah. Just ask his journalism students. They sold them for $1.50 at the school store for a newspaper fund raiser. They called him Mild Mannered English Teacher by day...Confectionery Magician by Night. And as for our slim trim Pamela, she does like her chocolate kisses, especially the ones with cherry centers.

I'm going to have the chance to be immersed in chocolate, though, as we are about to embark on another cruise. It features a midnight Chocolate Buffet. Since Bob doesn't stay awake that late, I fill a big plate with goodies for the two of us and we take them to breakfast the next morning to have with our milk. I hope he gets his share. I will allow myself to have three chocolate chip pancakes, with hot cocoa for breakfast. I will have two chocolate cookies with my chocolate ice cream at lunch. And at dinner I will limit myself to one slice of German chocolate cake with two scoops of chocolate ice cream on top.

Before bed, I plan to swipe the chocolate off Bob's pillow and replace it with a peppermint and if he doesn't smell my breath, I'll probably get away with it. By the time we get home I'll be so healthy and youthful from eating all that chocolate I'll never need to go to the fitness center again.

GREAT GREEN JELLO FIASCO

Where else but in Utah would you find a Great Green Jello Festival in the middle of the hot summer? Our church holds one every year, and this summer they added the incentive of a contest to see what can be made from Jello, green or otherwise. There is nothing like a contest to put my creative juices into overdrive.

I envisioned a peaceful summer fishing hole, so I dug out a large, 10 inch tall martini glass that had been used as a wedding decoration. It was big enough to hold at least two large packages of Jello. Since I was venturing into unknown territory, a trial run before Saturday would be in order.

I poured Nerds in the bottom to resemble gravel. Then I layered partially set green and blue Jello to the top. I carefully poked Swedish fish all around the sides and finished the whole creation off with a sign made of popsicle sticks that read, *"no fishin' allow'd."* It was a masterpiece!

I stored it in the refrigerator until Bob came home to admire it. He's my best fan. But wait! When it came out for display, the fish and the gravel had all turned dead white, and my cute little sign had sunk to the bottom of the bowl. Then, adding insult to injury, when a spoonful was taken out, a substance that looked and smelled like swamp water rushed in to fill the spoon hole. Bob was in stitches from laughing so hard. So much for my fan club.

Thomas Edison's first light bulb didn't work either, and I was determined to enter that contest. So I mixed my next batch just a couple of hours before the Festival. I wrapped the Nerds in clear plastic, so the Jello wouldn't contaminate them, and I hoped the kids that were sampling would not dig down into the bowl far enough to snag the plastic. I swirled the Jello in the bowl, but put the fish and the sign in my purse and off we went to celebrate green Jello.

On the table, the lady in charge had a plastic wading pool filled with ice to keep the Jello entries from melting. There were some very clever creations; marshmallows rolled in green Jello, green popcorn hearts with CTR written on them, and a small green train on a blue track with crumbled chocolate cookies as the dirt. I put my pond on the table, pushed the fish down into the Jello, stuck the sign in the middle, and wandered off to eat a hot dog. People were allowed to put a spoonful of each creation on their plate and vote for their favorite. My fishing hole seemed to be popular with the kids, but when I saw that the few remaining fish were beginning to turn white on their bottoms, I grabbed Bob and my fishing hole, and bugged out without waiting to see who won the prize. The prize was a box of green Jello, and I already have enough boxes at home for at least a year's supply.

I'm already planning next year's entry for the contest...a green Jello, life-sized bust of Al Gore. I hope global warming won't melt his nose off!

COOKING WITH JULIA

People ask me how the men in our family got to be such good cooks. Bob loves to make soups and salads. Dave likes to cook southern dishes like jambalaya and pecan pie. Rob, our grandson cooks gourmet foods like vegetables in Parmesan baskets and baklava. Bobby specializes in melt-in-your-mouth pancakes and barbecue. Our family dinners are feasts for kings, and they let the ladies eat also, if we wash the dishes.

I, on the other hand have single handedly been responsible for a series of culinary disasters. It began at age 12 when a girl friend and I decided to bake a cake to surprise my mother. This was in the days when there was no such thing as a cake mix in a box. There was special *Soft as Silk* cake flour that you sifted into the batter and we were careful to do all those things, but as the cake was baking we noticed a strange odor coming from the oven. The finished cake looked right although it was a little bit gray in color. But when mom got home she said, "What did you use for shortening?" Well, shortening was greasy and we had used the can of greasy bacon drippings mother always kept on the back of the stove. Big mistake! No one liked the bacon flavored cake we'd made.

In high school I tried again, making a delicious batch of Snickerdoodle cookies. This time I knew what shortening was, but I misread the measurements and put in a quarter *cup* soda instead of a quarter *teaspoon*. The cookies looked and smelled wonderful, but when you took a bite with a drink of milk, you foamed at the mouth like a rabid dog.

I headed out to college that next year and lived in the dorm where the meals were prepared for us, but every time I was home I practiced cooking. Still, even with mother's help, I turned out rolls that we used for hockey pucks, and runny soup that looked like dish water.

In my sophomore year at BYU my friends and I moved into the new Eliza R. Snow building where we had three bedrooms and a kitchen with all the works. We took turns cooking dinner, and I was determined to cook up something delicious. I found a great illustrated recipe in a magazine for Spam Peach Surprise. I sliced the Spam and put a peach half between each slice and poured the rest of the juice over the top. Then it went in the oven to brown. It looked crispy, and tasted almost adequate, but my roomies could not get their creative minds to accept a Spam and peach combination. They hid my *Julia Childs* magazines and teased me about the Spam the rest of the year.

By this time I realized I had to get serious about my cooking. Bob would be getting discharged from the Air Force at Christmas and I expected a proposal of marriage. So I took a cooking class. The bread, the puddings, the Eggs Benedict, all turned out perfectly, but I had lots of help. The girl in the cubicle next to mine was a returned missionary and a home economics major. She took it upon herself to supervise every thing I did. She earned me a B+ in the class.

When Bob came home, he did indeed ask my father for my hand, and was granted permission to marry me in June. I overheard Dad tell Mother, "Thank goodness! Now Jean can practice cooking on someone else and my ulcer will have a chance to heal."

Our first big Thanksgiving together I cooked a turkey, and made my aunt's special dressing casserole. After everyone left and Bob was cleaning up he said, "What is this inside the turkey?" He pulled out the paper package with the gizzard, heart, and neck inside. I was really surprised and said, "You expected me to stick my hand up there and do what?" Ever since that fiasco, Bob has cleaned and inspected the turkey before I'm allowed to cook it.

Since I've retired, I have adjusted my cooking expectations. I made some macaroons one day and left them in the oven too long. When I retrieved them they were dark brown. I hurriedly pushed a chocolate chip in the top of each one and tried to pass them off as chocolate macaroons. It might have worked too, except they were so hard Bob chipped a tooth.

After taking a microwave cooking class, I decided to mix up a batch of fudge for the family, who had all arrived home for Christmas. I thought I'd done everything right, but the darn stuff would not thicken up. Rather than toss it out, I added another bag of chocolate chips and stirred some more. Then I added another bag and another bag until I had a gigantic bowl of runny fudge. In desperation, I finally poured it all into quart jars, put a bow on top, and made a label that said, "Fun Fantasy Fudge Sauce" and sent the bottles home with the families after the holidays. Pam allowed that the flavor was good if you didn't mind the way it crunched on your teeth.

So now, when asked why the men in our family are such good cooks, I just smile and say, "Self preservation."

NIGHTTIME SERENADE

Since I frequently don't sleep well, I have become accustomed to the sounds of the night. No matter how hard I listen however, I've never heard some phantom singing opera. The closest I've come is hearing Bob as he snores...or more realistically, purrs. Many people, including my grand children think that people automatically become snorers after their 60th birthday, but that is not a fair assumption. Bob does not snore. He purrs. As for me, I don't ever hear a snore out of my mouth, although I frequently laugh in my sleep and that wakes me up.

The grand champion snorer in our family was my sweet Grandma Briggs. She was a tiny little lady, about five feet tall in her orthopedic shoes, but she could shake the rafters with a cacophony of sounds emitted from her throat, and magnified in a chamber that did not have teeth. For some reason when I was a kid, I was the one designated to sleep with her. I don't know if the grownups thought I was deaf, or I just didn't need much sleep, but it was always my duty. I got the dubious pleasure of being her bed companion at my house, at Aunt Marba's house, and even at Grandma's own house when there were sleep-overs. When she was in residence, I hurried to get to sleep before her serenade began. If I failed, I had to bounce back and forth on the bed until she rolled over on her side. Then if I was lucky and fast enough I could get to sleep before she rolled onto her back again. I missed her when she passed on, but I know she would be capable of shaking up the clouds in heaven.

We have a son-in-law who can belt out the midnight melodies with great gusto also. When he visits we put him in the basement bedroom under the kitchen, and if he's really in fine form, he can rattle the silverware in the drawers upstairs.

His wife has tried a number of anti-snore techniques and one was to sew a tennis ball to the back of his pajamas. That was to keep him sleeping on his side and not rolling over onto his back. But he was no princess and a tennis ball was not a pea. He just slipped off his pajama tops and slept like a baby...a very noisy baby.

I Googled the font of all knowledge for snoring remedies and found five pages of them. There were the jaw supports, and the Snore Ezzz pillows. Breathe Right Nasal Strips might do the trick, but they make your nose wide with a piggy flare. One site suggested changing sleep positions, losing weight, and avoiding alcohol. Your friendly neighborhood dentist can give you a product called Silent Nite. There was also a breath spray, or hypnosis. But the remedy to end all was a radio frequency needle to pierce the tongue, and was connected to a generator. Sounded like an Inquisition torture device meant to keep you awake for the rest of your life.

The thing that finally worked for our son-in-law was going to a sleep clinic. They found he had sleep apnea and he is now connected to a machine that feeds fresh air into his lungs at night. He has to wear a mask, and that machine whines and clicks all night, but now my silverware is safe.

As long as Bob and I have our own teeth and keep our snoring to a chuckle and a purr, we'll be content with that type of midnight serenade.

MUSCLES AND ME

You'd never guess by looking at me, but I spend a lot of time at the fitness center, building muscles...an interesting choice for an old duffer who might be more at home riding a recliner. Although I really suck at sports, I've tried to stay physically active ever since I threw myself into ballet lessons when Bob broke up with me in high school. I'd show him. I'd become a prima ballerina and dance with the Russian Ballet. He'd be sorry he missed his chance with a world famous dancer. So I stayed fit, as I danced my way through high school and then college.

Bob repented, and married me even though I was not famous nor Russian, and I became a school teacher instead. I still tried to stay fit. One evening after we were first married I was exercising and Bob looked down on my tense little face and said, "I bet I can do more sit ups than you!"

"Cannot," sez I.

"Can too. I'll bet you a dollar." Now in those days a dollar was a lot of money, especially for a couple of college students. I was up for the challenge. I hooked my toes under the couch and went at it. After twenty reps I was starting to weaken, but I got in five more by cheating a little. "There," I panted. "Can you do more than twenty five?"

"Nope, no. You win," he said, and put the money in my sweaty little hand and left the room chuckling to himself.

As our kids grew up my method of exercise changed. When Karen was married and had little kids, we took an aerobics class at six a.m., but when her family moved to Texas, there was no way I would get up alone at that hour. So I talked Bob into long walks in the evenings after school. This is not easy as Cedar City has many ups and downs, literally and figuratively. We always tried to walk down hill on the way home, when we were tired. Our neighbor Harold would call to us, "You do know that with all that walking you two are going to have to suffer seven years longer than the rest of us because we'll be dead, and you'll still be gimping around town."

In Highland, we walked with our little horses every day until the traffic got so busy around our street we were worried about their safety.

At sixty-something I was beginning to lose bone density, and a few miles from our home we found a fitness center that taught classes on weight lifting. With a little spinach, I thought I could become Ms. Popeye. I hated to go, but I felt so good afterward. It was like a shot of caffeine without the coffee. However, you are not supposed to lift two days in a row, so we continued our walking every other day until my knees gave out and Bob had to go solo.

When we moved to Draper, one of the first things we did was to find a good fitness center close to home, and there were a bunch of them. We settled on Dimple Dell because they seemed to like seniors. They had a contest from Thanksgiving to New Years, to *NOT* gain weight. I managed to keep off the weight and won a session with a trainer. He had me demonstrate my weight lifting techniques and pronounced them, "Awesome!" Now my only question is: If I'm so darn *awesome* at exercise, how come I'm not skinny like Olive Oil?

WOMAN OF MY AGE

This adventure in the life of *a woman my age* began a couple of years ago. Bob and I had an assignment to speak in church, and when we got home I confessed to having a little anxiety pain in my chest. Bob thought I should call the nurse's number that's listed on our insurance, because as we all know, most doctors do not work on Sunday. So I called, and described my little pain, and she strongly suggested that since I was in my 70's I should check in with an insta-care center. I said, "Yeah, yeah," and secretly decided to wait until Monday and call my own doctor. But in a few minutes the nurse phoned back and wanted me to call 911. *Women of my age* must be careful. "No way," I said, "but I will go to the insta-care center today."

So off we went, Bob and his book and me, grumbling all the way. The doctor on call said, "W*omen of your age* need to worry about heart attacks!" So they pasted a bunch of stickers on my chest, and wired me up to a machine...but everything looked fine. Then they did a chest x-ray and outside of a little scarring on my lungs, everything was in the right place. There was one blood test that would definitely determine if I were having a heart attack, but I would have to go to the ER for that.

X-rays in hand, off we went down the street to the ER. I signed in, but had to wait for a bed! "A bed," sez I! "I'm only here for a blood test."

"Oh, but we can't do just the blood test...*a woman your age* may be having a full-blown heart attack. You wouldn't be the first today." So they hooked me up to the wires again, did the blood test, and we waited half an hour until they could get the results. Still no sign of a heart attack. But do I get to go home? No, they paste a nitroglycerin patch on my chest, and tell me it might give me a serious headache. I already had a headache, called ER. They also gave me tablets to put under my tongue, and suggested I stay overnight in the hospital. They made an appointment with a cardiologist for me on Monday morning. Apparently cardiologists do not work on weekends either. Note to self: Do not have a heart attack on a weekend.

By this time it's four o'clock in the afternoon, and I have had no food nor drink since breakfast. My head was aching. I was determined to go home and I did! After I had lunch and calmed down, I packed my pajamas and went back to the hospital.

They said, "Whoa, you can't check yourself into the hospital, and the doctor who saw you has left for the day. We'll have to do the tests again."   By this time my arms looked like pin cushions and my chest was covered with red patches resembling a reticulated leopard, and my attitude was bad, *for a woman of any age!* This time they wanted a CAT scan, and I'm not even a cat. Finally at 9:30 p.m. a sympathetic woman doctor came in, and gave me encouraging news. "I can't find any signs of a heart attack. Why don't you go home, get a good night's sleep and check in with the cardiologist tomorrow. He works on Monday." I kissed her on both checks and got out of there as fast as my two little legs would go.

Bob and I spent Monday having more of the same tests, plus a stress test. The cardiologist came in with a big file of papers and said, "You have a very healthy heart, for *a woman of your age.* The thing causing you pain is an inflammation in your left lung, and a dose or two of Ibuprofen should take care of that in a couple of days...and it did. What a comedy of errors, but good news to know that I'm still going to be around for my 76th birthday, and *that is my age*! Next time I need the ER I'd better be unconscious, or I'm not going!

COLONOSCOPY-THEY PUT *WHAT* UP *WHERE?*

As we grow older there comes a time when your primary care physician mentions the dreaded **C** word...that's right, *colonoscopy.* You remember, that's where they take a TV camera and lights (the size of a Mini Cooper), and push it up your backside so high that it televises your stomach and what you had for breakfast. Oh, wait. You didn't have any breakfast, or lunch, or dinner because you've been on a 24-hour fast. I've been the recipient of seven of these dubious exams, but this time it was Bob's turn for the fun and games.

As bad as the colonoscopy is, it doesn't compare with the preparation for said procedure. You go to the drug store and tell them what you're going to have done. After they finish smirking, they hand over a full gallon bottle with a mysterious white powder in the bottom, and four pages of instructions. First, there is a list of medications you cannot take for a week before, and then there is a list of low fiber foods you must eat for three days, and then it gets bad. The day before, you can only eat or drink things that are transparent...delicious things like yellow Jello, and broth, and the ever ready 7 Up.

At noon, when your stomach is so empty that it thinks your throat is cut, you fill that plastic bottle with cold water and begin to gulp, *not sip,* it down. It tastes so bad, it must have been invented as a torture by witch doctors to keep away the evil spirits. The smell is like salty swamp water, it slides down your throat like slime. You drink half the bottle and then wait, preferably near the bathroom because before long your stomach and intestines begin to rock and roll and you begin the potty run! It gets worse and you think an atomic reaction is building inside you. As that continues, you begin to get a little shaky and your stomach gets nauseous, and when you go into the bathroom, you don't know which end to hang over the potty; your backside or your face. In about four hours your body begins to adjust and then it's time for you have to ingest the rest of the witch stuff in big gulps, and the rush to the bathroom begins anew. Bob spent so much time sitting on the potty, that he had a big red ring on his backside that the doctor used as a target so he knew exactly where to put the TV camera.

We prefer to do ugly tasks early in the morning. Bob says, "If you have to swallow a frog, don't sit and stare at it all day," so we were at the West Endoscopy Center at seven a.m. This is big business these days, and there were about eight beds filled with people, all having colonoscopies. They were rolling people in and out of there as fast as they could and they don't let any vertical-standing people in the back until the procedure is done. I think they don't want anyone to escape. They had Bob remove his pants and shoes, and a nurse put a needle in his hand and wheeled him in to see the doctor. Bob said he was talking to the doctor, a very tall brown athletic type, and all of a sudden he was out, and that was all he remembered until we got home.

Before we left, the doctor talked to me and gave me colored pictures of the insides of Bob's colon. They can go in his scrapbook with the pictures of the inside of his skull they took in April and pictures of his legs when they stripped his veins. We'll have enough information and DNA that we can clone him for future generations. They gave me papers to sign testifying that I would take good care of Bob and not feed him any beans or soda pop for the rest of the day, and they wheeled him out to the car and I drove home. When we got home he keep asking, "Are they finished yet?" I rolled him into bed and he only woke up to drink milk and eat a Krispie Kreme doughnut.

The good news after all that ickfulness is that Bob has a beautiful colon, and does not have to have the dreaded **C** for another 10 years...that will make him almost 90, and by then who cares how his colon looks?

COLDS AND MOORE COLDS

Will someone please explain to me why, with all the modern miracles in medicine, we still don't have a cure for the common cold? Maybe this is God's way of making sure we can exercise the "sickness and health" clause in our marriage contract. This is the third cold I've had this year, and I just don't get over the darn things like I used to. I think I caught it on the airplane coming home from Tampa. Airplanes can be rather germy. So when I started to feel lousy, I began sucking on those Cold Ease tablets. Cold *Ease*, nothing...they made a sore in the top of my mouth. Then I tried a decongestant that sapped all my energy. My head feels like it's encased in a glass fish bowl and all the sounds ring in my ears. There is a circle of hurt around my eyes. My throat is scratchy, and my chest feels squishy, and that's not easy when you have a chest the size of mine. Now I just sit in my fuzzy bathrobe and warm socks and gloves, soaking down hot liquids, which is a trick in itself because I have tissues stuffed up both nostrils. I rub my chest with Vick's medicated stuff *with vaporizing cold medicine,* and wrap one of Bob's wool scarves around my neck.   I am truly a sight to behold, (on Halloween, maybe). I nap two or three times a day, because I can't sleep well at night. My coughing wakes me up. This all makes me very crabby.

I hate colds, not as much as stomach flu, but this is miserable! When I was little, my momma would mix up a concoction called a mustard plaster, spread it between two pieces of an old towel like a medicinal sandwich, and put it on my bare chest. Then I had to lay there with no wiggling while the mess heated up until my skin became sun-burned red. She peeled it off and carefully stashed it in the trash so it wouldn't get on her fingers, and spread on a purple paste called Musterole. I don't know what was in that, but it made my eyes water and my nose burn. Lastly she would wrap my throat in flannel rags and pronounce me cured.

However, if I should dare produce a cough, she had a brew for that too. It was made of honey and lemon juice and, I suspect, a bit of spirits. It was really nasty, so I tried to hold my cough in as long as possible, but at first hack, out came the brew.

A couple of months after Bob and I were first married, we were working in Nevada to earn our tuition to go back to BYU. We were sharing a cold, as newly weds we shared everything, and we decided to share a hot toddy. We really didn't know what a hot toddy was, but did hear it was great for knocking out a cold. So we bought some booze, and poured it in some lemonade, heated the whole thing up and drank it right down. Well, it worked alright! We were so busy throwing up the rest of the night, we didn't even feel the cold anymore. No more alcohol for these Moores.

Fifty years ago, a bad cold would last seven days, or with doctor's care...a week. But not now. Oh, no. Now that I'm officially old, I've been coughing and hacking for three weeks and it shows no signs of letting up.

So far I've missed my art class, my mammogram, a play at the Desert Star Playhouse, a family history class, a fireside, and church, twice. They'll introduce me as a newcomer when I can attend once more. Did I mention I'm also crabby?

If I were the vindictive type, I'd drag my germy body over to visit all the neighbors I don't like and cough in their doorway. But since I don't have any neighbors I don't like, I'll just keep all this misery to myself. I realize it's not terminal.

P.S. How come Bob did not catch cold?

SHINGLES-NOT THE ROOF KIND

Shingles are painful, and I cannot think of anything that's the least bit funny about them.

INSIDE BOB'S HEAD

About ten years ago I let some salesman sweet talk me into buying a mattress pad that was impregnated with 500 ceramic magnets that were supposed to cure bunions, pink eye, and everything in between. So except for sore knees and few minor aches and pains, Bob and I have been fairly healthy. But I'm beginning to think our wondrous pad is losing its umph.

Wednesday, Bob woke me up about eight a.m. to tell me he was going to the doctor's office. He had been feeling a little dizzier than usual. I told him to go quietly, rolled over on my magnets, grateful that I would not have to go to the fitness center, and I went back to sleep.

I finally regained consciousness about nine and went into the living room to find our grand daughter Katie, sniffing and sneezing and curled up in a reclining chair in front of the fireplace with a temperature of 102 degrees. It was her 17th birthday too, so I did my maternal duty and fixed her a glass of instant breakfast, toast, grapes, and a vitamin C pill.

Just then the phone rang. "Is this Mrs. Moore?"

"Yes, but I don't want to buy anything."

"Is your husband named Robert?"

"Yes, but I already own him."

"You don't understand. This is Dr. Morse's nurse and he is here, but the doctor doesn't think he should be driving. Can you come pick him up?"

I threw on some clothes, grabbed my purse, and asked Katie to drive me and bring Bob's car home. But when we got to the door it was snowing like crazy and Katie was in a blanket, but with no shoes. So I sent her back to her chair and found one of our neighbors at home and willing to take me to the doctor's office.

When I walked in, there sat my Bob with band aids on his finger and on his arm. I said, "Come on, Honey...I'll take you home."

But the doctor said, "Oh no you don't. We think he's had a small stroke and he has an appointment at the Stroke Center right now."

I called Katie to see if she would be all right, and off we went in the snow, with me driving and Bob mumbling that he was perfectly capable of operating a car.

For all the anxiety exhibited at Dr. Morse's office, nobody seemed in a hurry at the Stroke Center. After filling out all the papers they called our insurance company to see if we were covered before they started treatment. No freebies here. I sat in the waiting room for about an hour and then sneaked back to the inner sanctum to see what was going on. There was Bob all laid out with his head in a machine that kept moving him in and out, shaking his brain down to the bottom of his skull. They assured me he was fine, so I sat down back in the waiting room for another half hour and then went back to check again. This time he was in a chair and they had some kind of a machine on his head that looked like a reject from Dr. Frankenstein's lab, and I was sure they were trying to turn his brain into green Jello.

It was getting to be lunch time by then, so I called Katie again. She was a princess holding court. One friend had brought her soup, bread, chocolate covered strawberries...and three aspirin. Her dad had brought over a big bouquet of flowers. Three of her girl friends had come with presents, birthday cake, and balloons. She was feeling no pain which was better than me, as I had had nothing to eat all day.

My third time in to see Bob was the charm. He was just sitting up like a good boy waiting for the doctor to come in. He had a wicked looking shunt in his arm so they could inject tiny robots to float around in his blood and eat up all the green Jello that leaked out from his brain. The Doctor Lady was very thorough and felt 94% sure that he had experienced a mini-stroke with no damage, but she wanted more tests.

So the rest of the week was spent going from one test to another while they poked, pricked, and scanned poor Bob. One of the tests was a 24-hour heart monitor that involved taping wires on his front and back, and wearing a little box around his waist. When we got home I tried to convince him that he was really a giant dot to dot puzzle, but when I went for my Magic Markers he escaped to the bathroom and refused to come out. We were a little bit afraid that our magnetic mattress would cause the recording to stop when Bob went to bed, but I guess those little robots kept things moving right along.

We went in for the final diagnosis and except for the mini-stroke he is a very healthy 77 year old man. The worse part came when we went to pick up his Plavix to prevent anymore strokes, and the bill came to $147 for 30 pills. If you're money smart, that comes to $5 a day for those little suckers. Ah, the high cost of staying healthy, but when you consider the alternative what can you do? I'll gladly keep him around for a few Moore years.

GROWING A NEW FACE

I'm not sure why Bob has to visit the dermatologist *every* year. The doctor is a pretty lady with a flawless complexion, but he may just be concerned about his own grizzled old hide, who knows? This year's visit uncovered some big problems. His feet had grown some large, hard callouses on the bottom and there were some basal cell skin cancers forming on his face.

The feet were an easy fix. His kindly wife, me, sandpapered them, rubbed them with Vick's Vaporub, and encased them in clean soft socks every night.

The face was a little trickier. For one month Bob had to rub Carac cream on his face morning and night. The first week his face got pink, like the blush of an embarrassed school girl. By the second week his forehead, temples and cheeks were as bright red as a slice of fried ham. During the third week dark purple spots had formed on the red fried ham, and every morning his eyes were almost swollen shut. He looked like a frog peeking through the ice. I got worried, and called the doctor's office to see if the swelling was normal. It was. It's an itchy proposition and with his feet in hot socks and a burning tender face, he was having trouble sleeping soundly.

It was even more trouble going out in public. Some people just stared and the more adventurous souls asked what had happened. Bob, always ready with a colorful story said, "We came upon an accident just off the freeway. There was this little child trapped in a burning car, and I went to the rescue. Just as the two of us got out, the car exploded in my face. Didn't you see us on the six o'clock news?" That story felicitated a lot of sympathy...and I'm supposed to be the story teller of this family.

By the fourth week the outer layer of skin on his face had dried up and started to slough off. I could always track Bob by the trail of skin he left wherever he went. It was like living inside a snow globe. Then things really got bad. His poor old skin started to crack and bleed. I was afraid his face was going to fall off, and I'm fond of that face. I insisted he go to the doctor's office. The doctor was delighted to see him! "That's exactly how your face is supposed to look," she said. She took pictures and called all of her staff in to admire my husband's burning face. "Now you can stop with the Carac and start with the healing cream." She didn't even charge him for the impromptu visit.

After the two months of burning and peeling were over, a brand new layer of skin began to appear. We nourished it with cream and moisturizers and it was smooth as a baby's behind without the age spots and wrinkles he used to have. The kids thought he looked twenty years younger, which meant he was married to an older woman. I was not jealous. Maybe I should try the old Carac treatment too. When he reported to Dr. Hottie for his six month check up, she pronounced him beautiful from head to toe, or face to foot, if you prefer.

FACIALS AND FANCY LIVING

A couple of years ago, we were on an LDS Church History tour, and one of the places we stayed was a very elegant resort. Our accommodations included a sitting room with a couch and big screen TV, and a separate bedroom. The bed itself was huge and piled high with pillows, and a soft mattress that was about a yard off the floor. Now then, 36 inches high to people with normal legs is not bad, but when your whole self is only 59 inches high, big problem because the mattress was waist high to little old me. Could I get up?

I didn't worry, so when Bob went to bed, I stayed up to watch TV and perform my bedtime rituals. I brushed my teeth, washed my face, and applied a generous portion of lotion to same. Then I sat down to watch the end of my TV show. Soon my face began to burn and itch something awful, and when I couldn't stand it any longer, I ran to the mirror. Staring back at me was a bright red face that seemed to glow in the dark. I grabbed the little complimentary bottle of lotion I had used and found that I had rubbed shampoo into my funny little, and now tender, face. I turned on the water and rinsed several times, but each rinsing brought a new layer of foam, and new tears to my eyes. After I finally wiped away all the foam, I carefully rubbed Vaseline all over my face, figuring by then my skin could use a little moisture.

Bob was asleep when I finally made it in to bed; as he's almost asleep as soon as his head hits the pillow. I didn't want to disturb him, but at this point that bed looked awfully high. Since my backside did not reach the top of the mattress, I tried laying on my back and pushing my feet against the wall. No way! The wall was too far from the bed.

My next effort was to stand at the foot of the bed, fall forward and drag my little self up to sleeping position. That did work until it came to getting onto my sore knees, and then I had to roll off to the side before my moaning woke up Bob. But he slept blissfully on, unaware that his wife was in *big* trouble.

By now I was getting desperate, so I grabbed hold of his hand. He snorted and tried to pull away, but I hung on with all my might, and he pulled me right onto the bed, like landing a fish. "What are you doing?" he mumbled in his sleepy condition.

"Just getting into bed."

"Well, its about time," he said as he rolled over and commenced with his heavy breathing again. I settled in for a long sleep, hoping that I wouldn't have to get down and grease my sore face again in the middle of the night.

Travel went on as usual the next day, although my face felt like sandpaper, but then who was going to come up and feel my face? If they got that close I could always bite them, right? On the second day came the real kicker, as my face began to peel. It took about five days to complete the process.

Well, I learned something new through that experience. I know how to get a chemical face peel without the expense of a dermatologist.

DO YOU SEE WHAT EYE SEE?

Senior citizens usually enjoy a little excitement in their lives, and there is nothing that adds excitement more than letting a surgeon cut into your eyeball. About fifteen years ago, during a routine exam for new glasses, the doctor said casually, "Oh...by the way, you're developing cataracts." After he pried my anxious little hands off of his necktie, he added, "but you won't have to worry about them for many years." My aunt Helen had cataract surgery when I was just a kid and they put sandbags on each side of her head and made her lie perfectly still for a week. Oww!

I just put the whole thing in the back of my mind and tried to forget about sandbags, but each time I went in for new glasses they would politely remind me about the cataracts. I was hoping if I didn't acknowledge them, they would just disappear. They really didn't bother me...yet.

Then when we were in Hawaii, I began to notice big halos around all the lights at night and they blurred out everything else. When we went looking for a specific address, Bob would say, "What is the name on that street sign?" I squinted, blinked hard, and said, "What street sign?" In the bright light of day, I had a hard time distinguishing the color of traffic lights. I was also finding it hard to read, and I love to read. But since we were returning stateside in a month, I decided to wait to get my eyes checked.

Within a week of returning home, I shuffled into the optometrist's office for new specs. They were stylish, but didn't help much. My sweet little Katie ratted on me and told her mother I had to ask the color of the traffic lights when I was driving. The family came to a unilateral decision, and I was no longer allowed to drive, day or night! They confiscated my car keys. It was time to go for a second opinion about those cataracts.

It was a Friday when we drove to the fancy Eye Institute, where an optometrist gave me a thorough eye exam. I thought I was doing a great job reading the eye chart, but when I looked over at Bob he had his hand over his mouth to stifle a laugh. At one point they turned off all the lights and asked me to read the sentences on a little card. "What card?" sez I.

The doctor said, "I think it's time to have something done about those cataracts." I was excited when I found they could also put a corrective lens right inside my eye that would give me 20/20 vision. I wouldn't have to wear glasses anymore! I've worn glasses since I was twelve years old, and for just a few hundred dollars more I could pitch the glasses. Nobody would call me "four-eyes" anymore. I could wear a pair of those fancy designer sun glasses that you buy right off the rack!

Before I had time to worry, they scheduled surgery for the right eye on Monday, and the left eye one week later. They gave me a long list of instructions and sent me home to prepare.

Monday, in comfortable clothes, and after a light breakfast, we appeared at the appointed time. I filled out and signed a grundle of papers. Then they gave me a Valium, a cap, a gown, and booties, and laid me out in a dentist chair. They put several kinds of drops in my little blue eye, and through blurry vision, I met Dr. Crandall for the very first time. In my best drug-induced language, I told him how important my 72 year-old eyes were to me. On my chest they set a little pump with a tube that blew air into my face, but it kept sliding off. It must have been designed by men for men with flat chests. As I pushed it back in place, the nurse said, "Don't do that, you're not sterile."

"I certainly hope not," the Valium said, trying to be funny, but nobody laughed but me.

Next they covered my entire body with a heavy plastic sheet, all except for my right eye. By then everything was a blur, which was good, because I was unable to see the instruments coming at me. The colors and patterns I did see were beautiful...sometimes red rectangles, blue circles or sometimes colors just floating around. What an awesome laser show! The entire surgery took about ten minutes.

When it was over, I sat contentedly in the waiting room for Bob to come get me. He had been watching everything on TV. The nurse brought three different kinds of drops for my eye, and a pair of cool wrap-around sun glasses, and sent me home. That night I had to wear a plastic eye patch that made me look like a cyclops. The next day I went back to the clinic and actually got to talk to the surgeon for about thirty seconds. He pronounced that my right eye passed with flying colors. It was so exciting to see how bright and beautiful the world had become.

A week later I went through the whole process again on my left eye, and now with two fancy eye patches I can be a lady bug for Halloween. I hope the Lion's Club will take my collection of old eye glasses.

The only down side to this whole experience is when I look in the mirror in the morning. I wonder *who* that wrinkled old lady is, and *why* in the heck is she wearing my pajamas?

MY SWINGIN' KNEES

After gimping along for ten years on arthritic knees, I finally bit the bullet and had my left knee replaced. It was "brutal" surgery, and the first day I thought I was going to die. The second day I was hoping I would die. But on the third day they promised to let me go home to a comfortable bed and good meals, so I decided to go on living. The first couple of hours in the hospital were pure bliss and then I came to my senses, almost. I had tubes in almost every orifice of my little body including the oxygen tubes up my nose.

"Do you need morphine?" asked the nurse.

"Yes, please...all I can get," I murmured in my drug-induced haze.

"I have a shot for you," nurse Hurts-a-lot said. "I have to give it to you in your stomach."

"You and what army," sez me, knowing that resistance was futile. It was just a little prick, and to be honest, with all the other stuff going on, it was not that bad. Then she hoisted my wounded limb up on the *torture machine* that was designed to bend said limb back and forth for three hours. I thought the darn thing was going to pull my leg out by the roots. Two hours was my limit before I hollered "uncle*!*"

Then came the biggest torture of all...lunch! She pulled the tray in front of my chin, taped a spoon to my hand, and said, "Enjoy." It was a brown something on a piece of bread with a brown sauce, accompanied by canned green beans, milk, juice and a brownie that had been smashed under a saucer. It didn't taste very good, but I was much too weak to barf. After a while, nurse Hurts-a-lot came in and asked, "Is that all your going to eat?" I drank the milk didn't I? That's not good enough?

Without a break in came the physical therapist. "Would you like to stand up?" he asks, cheerfully.

"Would you like to have this spoon shoved up your nose?" I answered. But I was determined to do what I was asked, so I stood up, like a flag waving in the breeze, and that was just my hospital gown. Those lovely gowns were designed by Mr. Seymour Butts. By the third day they were making me walk down the hall to the stairs and the therapist taught me how to get up and down stairs so I could get into my own house.

Being in the hospital to rest is an oxymoron. They woke me up at five a.m. every morning to put me on the torture machine, so I would be ready for my delicious lump of breakfast at seven. Then came the physical therapist and the respiratory therapist to put me through my paces, so to speak. The doctor, a family friend, would peek in from time to time, and cheerfully tell me how much better my knee was now that he had cleaned out all of the spurs and rough edges. It's good I had the worst one done first, now the second one wouldn't be so bad, I hoped. After three days of hard work and bad food, Dr. Wells released me to come home. Finally, I get to rest. Not! Bob still had to give me shots in my stomach twice and day, and they sent that darn torture machine home so I could practice three times a day. Bob and David hoisted me up the stairs, and I gimped into bed for a nap.

The PT came to our home and convinced me that bending that knee would hurt less than holding it out straight in front of me. Who would have guessed it? Once on familiar ground, I quickly advanced from walker, to crutches, to cane, and when I wanted to see people gasp, I used nothing but my two little feet. After three weeks there was actually very little pain anymore, except a zinger now and then from the cutting edge. I managed the discomfort with Aleve and sometimes a sleeping pill at night.

Twelve days later Bob loaded me into the car and off we went to get the stitches out. I had considered taking a tranquillizer before going, and the nurse said, "It's too bad you didn't."

"Wait a minute, and I'll go home and get one. It's only 30 miles,"

"Too late," she said and grabbed a stitch end, twisted it around the pliers, and started to slowly pull. I held onto my incision because I was sure she was ripping it out, twelve inches at a time, but Bob told me the first piece was only about four inches long. There were three other pieces, but by then I was numb and they were not so bad.

The doctor came in and was amazed at how well I was doing. He said I could be his poster girl for quick recovery. He sent me back to the fitness center and told me to take up all my usual activities, except for housecleaning, laundry, and cooking. Okay, I made that last part up myself but it sounds good.

Now I've actually grown to prefer my new knee because it's so dependable. I lead with that leg as I climb up the stairs. I do get tired easily and have to shower and do my toilette in phases. I take lots of little cat naps and I'm not even a cat, and Bob pampers me and feeds me good meals. I'm doing so well that I'm ready to get a part time job at IHOP.

PART TWO

Three months to the day after my first surgery, I had my right knee replaced. I wrote a note on my knee that said, "Dr. Wells, we've got to quit meeting like this. I'm running out of knees." He had a big laugh and insisted the sign stay put until his surgery staff had a chance to read it. I guess there are not a lot of laughs in the operating room.

So now I have two Striker titanium alloy knees, with cobalt tips and guaranteed not to rip, tear, wrinkle or turn up on the edges. It was still very painful, and if I had my way, they could just keep me drugged for a month until the pain ceased and the stitches were out, but it was not to be.

Two weeks out of the hospital, Pam, who was visiting us, decided I needed to get out for some fresh air. I was still on crutches, but we have a Kohl's Department store nearby and we had coupons. So off we went. We got inside, and there by the door was a wheel chair just waiting for me. Pam plopped me down, put my crutches on either side, and laid our purses on my lap. Pam does a lot of things very well, but pushing wheel chairs is not one of them. She promptly ran my right foot into the corner of a display counter. My knee was not happy, so I positioned my crutch over the edge of my toe like a bumper. That took care of *that* problem.

Next she wheeled me through the clothes racks, and the hangers and the clothes caught onto the wheel chair and my crutches. When we got back to the aisle, Pam had to dig through the clothes to find me. When we quit laughing, she put all the clothes back on the rack, and parked my wheel chair by the cash register. Pam took off and I waited and waited until I got bored, so I played tag with a couple of little toddlers who walked faster than I could wheel.

When she was ready to go, Pam retrieved me and we paid for our goods, returned the chair, and I gimped out the door with my crutches, my plastic bags and my purse hung around my neck like a hood ornament. I came home happy but tired and ready for a nap.

The new knees did not make me any taller, but I am no longer bow-legged. I walk almost like a real person now, and I'm glad I had it done. I'm even more grateful that I only have two knees instead of four.

THERAPIST OR TERRORIST?

I've been told that the difference between a therapist and a terrorist is this: You can negotiate with a terrorist. A physical therapist started working on me a couple of hours after knee surgery, and it is ongoing. The PT came into my hospital room and said, "It's time to stand up on your new knee!" That wasn't a question, it was a statement. If I had been strong enough I would have smacked him with my ice pack, but he just stood there waiting and the only way I could get him to leave is to do what he asked. So moaning and groaning, I stood up.

"Now take a step," he said. That wasn't a question either, so I took a step back and sat down on the bed again. "Alright," he said. "I guess that will do for now." But did he leave me alone? Definitely not! He kept showing up in my room twice a day.

Did I get rid of him when I got home? Definitely not...he sent a friend to bug me. My new PT, Damon, would bend my leg back until it hurt. "Now hold that for 15 seconds," sez he. My 15 second counts were much shorter than his, but then it wasn't his leg bent under him at 110 degrees either.

Damon is a good man with an enthusiastic smile and a great hand shake, and he worked my wounded knee so I could have a normal range of motion and less scarring. He made the impossible things become possible with a little ache and pain. I know of people who had called it quits after a painful therapy session, but Bob wouldn't let me beg off, and Damon kept knocking on my door.

When my stitches were removed, the doctor said I could go back to the fitness center. As soon as they ran my membership card, they discovered I was no longer homebound, and canceled my home therapy. Like a little lost puppy I followed my Damon to his office. He would continue to work with my new knee and I would still have to stretch and hold it.

The first thing he did was to wrap my knee in a giant heating pad and cook it. It felt so good that now I get him to wrap both my knees. This is kind of a Shake and Bake process where the bake comes first. Then he shakes my leg and bends my knee until it really really hurts, and then tells me to hold it for 15 painful seconds. He measures the angle, and if it isn't bent enough, we do the shake stuff again. He's hoping for 110 degrees, and I'm hoping it won't break off like peanut brittle. He also presses my knee down to a flat 0 degrees...another 15 seconds of hurt.

My next trick is on the slant board, no not the water board. I do ten minutes of foot raises, ten minutes of toe raises, and ten minutes of heel tucks. I'm ready for a nap, but Damon insists I do hamstring curls with 20 pound weights.

After an hour of lifts, bends and shakes, I'm ready for electrical stimulation and that's my favorite part. Damon sticks little magnetic squares connected to electrical wires all around my knee and turns on the electricity. He puts an ice pack over everything, and I say a little prayer that the water doesn't leak onto the electrical wires and fry my knee cap. My knee tingles and tickles and I giggle my time away until the timer goes off and I'm done. I'd like to say that Bob and I then go to the fitness center to work the rest of my body, but I'm so tired I just go home, curl up in my favorite chair and watch Tuner Classic Movies until Bob serves me my lunch.

I'll miss Damon for about 15 seconds when my therapy is over, but I sure won't miss the stretching.

IPOD EXPERIENCE

I have a new toy...or perhaps it has me, I'm not sure. After my experience with knee surgery, I decided I needed an iPod to encourage my walking. There's nothing like a little "Onward Christian Soldiers" to cover up the sounds of my moaning as I gimp around the neighborhood. So the family electronics guru, Rob, went on line and found me a fancy hot pink model with lots of memory.

When it arrived I laid it by the computer until another grandkid, Andrea, came by and showed me what to do with the cute little thing. The first trick she did was to take videos with it. I haven't mastered that yet, so I have to look at Andrea and me mugging for the camera until I learn to put something else on video, hence that part of my iPod controls itself for now.

Next we registered the iPod, and downloaded a music site on my computer. I named it Jean's Music. Not very creative I know, but it had to have a name that I could remember. My memory doesn't have the megabytes of an iPod.

I gathered all my CD's, brushed off the dust, and my "geek squad" showed me how to *rip* them. They just did three albums because they had other commitments, and they turned the *ripping* part over to me. I succeeded in getting them on my computer, but not onto my iPod. Then it came to me. You must have the iPod plugged into the computer. You'll be happy to know that I have now become an expert *ripper*.

I have a great music assortment on my iPod; classical, Christmas, religious, folk songs and even some Marty Robbins in case Bob ever wants to sneak a listen.

I found that the little round earphones that came with my iPod made my ears sore, and I have enough sore stuff on my old body for now, so I took a trip to Best Buy to see what they had to offer brand new iPod owners. It was prodigious. Many different kinds of earphones, stands, speakers, and iPod carriers. I did get some comfortable earphones, but Andrea said, "Don't buy a carrier, Gram. Just stick it in your bra." Always anxious to save a penny, I decided to give my bra a try. When we headed to the fitness center the next morning, my iPod with 349 songs came with me tucked in my bra. It was rather a tight fit, and when I got there I decided to change songs. I tried to pull it out, but succeeded only in disconnecting the earphones while it played the *Hallelujah Chorus* inside my bra. Well, then I had to stick my hand down inside my shirt and fish the darn thing out. I looked around and a few ladies were chortling, and the men were thinking, "What the heck?" I decided that the *in the bra* option is just not for me, so I came home and crocheted a little pink granny bag that hangs around my neck and looks girlie, but it works.

Now if I could just get it to play the music I want. It seems to have a mind of its own, and when I turn it on, it starts playing the theme from *Close Encounters,* and I didn't even download that. I poke at the dial, and sometimes get what I want, and sometimes it just shuts itself off. I wonder if I've lost control and entered into the *Twilight Zone.*

Looking at the menu, when I can find it, there are a lot of things listed that I don't understand. Things like photos, podcasts, radio, and extras. What is a podcast anyway? Maybe I'm sending signals into outer space, and aliens will come to visit me and my bra in Draper. They had better be *legal* aliens, or there will be some ripping problems.

WRINKLES OF TIME

We live in a time where most folks worship youth and beauty. As senior citizens, we have neither. Oh yea, there's always that inner beauty stuff, but it's hard to see it under all our wrinkles. When we were babies, parents loved our little wrinkles of fat. They tickled them and rubbed them with lotion. But nobody loves them now...not even us. When I was twenty I began getting little *laugh* wrinkles on my forehead and around my eyes. I tried putting tape on them at night, and in the morning they were smoothed out. That only lasted until I moved my face muscles and they popped right back into place. As I grew older I tried many kinds of creams and ointments, but wrinkles just kept gathering like ants at a picnic. Now in my late 70's, I not only have horizontal wrinkles, but some vertical wrinkles have crept in also. There are some above my eyebrows, but the two deepest run from the corners of my mouth down to my chin. The depth allows saliva to run down and drip off my chin, if I don't swallow fast enough. If I eat something chocolate, it makes brown rivulets down my chin. That is not very attractive, except to a family dog who likes to lick faces, if I had a family dog.

But wrinkles are not the only pesky growths on the aging skin. Take the hanging moles that grow around my neck...please. I go to the dermatologist every couple of years and have them harvested. She takes her little scissors and just clips them off. If I didn't get that done I would undoubtedly have a ring around my neck. Every time I wanted to go out I could paint them to look like pearls, but that would be a pain in the neck. Or I could always wear a turtle neck sweater to match my turtle neck skin.

Hair seems to grow wild on senior skin. I can't seem to get enough on my head, but I can grow it on my chin and top lip. I could become the bearded lady if I didn't submit to a monthly hot wax job. Men grow hair in odd places too, mostly in their ears and noses. Sometimes it looks like they're growing nests for small birds inside their ears. And plucking hair out of the nose is a painful process. It makes your eyes water.

Then there are the warts and barnacles. Warts are easy to get rid of. You cut a potato in half, rub it on the wart...oh, wait. That was my grandmother's recipe. Now days you just put a piece of duct tape over the offending wart for a week, and when you pull it off and the oxygen-deprived wart comes off too. Barnacles are a different breed, and my dermatologist says don't worry about them. A lot she knows. I don't see any on her arms or legs.

Bruises are now big and red and very easy to come by. They look awful, but they don't last more than 14 days or two weeks.

Sun spots seem to pop out on my arms and legs like freckles, only bigger. As I get older and get more sun spots, will they all melt in together and give me a lovely olive completion? Suntan, here I come.

The rich and famous have found solutions to all these little quirks, but sometimes at the cost of sanity. Many of them look like they've been encased in plastic, and if they move their lips to speak their whole face will crack open. Consequently, they speak like ventriloquists, barely moving their lips. Also, I have a problem with Botox. Isn't that a poison? If you get enough in your system, will your nose or ears fall off? I'm suspicious.

With all this other stuff going on, our aging bodies get the flops. My chin has two flops that resemble drapery down the front of my neck. My upper arms have flops that wave in the breeze when I conduct the music in church. My boobs, stomach,

and behind all hang low. Even my poor little ankles. I looked
down at my feet the other day and said, "My pantyhose are
wrinkled around my ankles. I need to pull them up tighter." But it
wasn't my hose at all. It was my wrinkled ankles. Maybe if I get
rich and famous I'll have a face lift and get rid of all the flops. But
I'm afraid they'd have to pull my skin so tight my belly button
would become a dimple in my chin, and I'd hate to guess what
those things hanging from my ears are. For now, I'll just endure
my wrinkles, flops, and sun spots.

BURYING BONNIE

Sometimes its hard to put loved ones to rest...especially if they're just an ash. Take the trials of my friend Jane. She has a unique place in her family as the youngest of nine children. She was well cared for by her parents and siblings, and now in her mid seventies, she has the responsibility of being the care giver for her older frail family members. Such it was with her sister Bonnie.

Bonnie was a beautiful young lady when she married Tom, who was handsome and rich. He had made a fortune inventing sports equipment, and so they lived in Sun Valley with their only son, Jason. Tom lost that fortune, but had another invention up his sleeve that net him another fortune. As he grew older, that fortune disappeared too, and son Jason decided to seek his own fortune in California as *Boon Doggie, the silver haired surfer.*

As Tom and Bonnie grew older they needed help caring for themselves and settled into an assisted living facility in Sun Valley. Tom grew ill and died before he could come up with another fortune and he was cremated and his ashes scattered on his beloved ski slopes. That left Bonnie all alone with no kith or kin in Sun Valley.

Jason wanted to take his mother to California, but the high cost of assisted living homes there was prohibitive. So he decided to take her to Salt Lake City. The prices were reasonable and most of her siblings were living in the area. This is where Jane and husband Karl come into the picture again. They lived in Provo, but every week they would make the forty minute trip to see Bonnie, fix her hair, clean her room and take her shopping. This loving care went on for about seven years, and finally Bonnie's time had come. Jason drove in from California, and Jane and Karl came up from Provo to say farewell, and gather up Barbara's belongings.

When she passed on, they asked what Jason wanted to do. Jason said, "I don't know. I think I'd like to have her cremated and take her to California, but I don't have any money. Besides, I have to get home. Surf's up!"

Tender-hearted Jane said, "We'll find the money to take care of her," as Karl was shaking his head. So they called around and found the best price was a place in Provo, and the deal was made.

Three weeks went by and they had not heard anything. They called the mortuary and the man said, "Oh yeah. I went up to Salt Lake to pick up the remains, but the death certificate was not signed, so they wouldn't release her."

Jane called Salt Lake. "Well," they said. "The attending physician has left the country and we're not sure when he'll be back."

"You mean there is no one up there who can ascertain she is dead and sign the certificate? She's been laying in a cooler for three weeks! I'll send my brother up, he's a doctor...a PhD."

"Never mind...we'll find someone," they said apologetically.

Another two weeks went by with no word about Bonnie, when Jane answered a knock at her door. There stood the mortician with a small cardboard box tied with a big black bow. "I feel so badly about the delay," he said, "I decided to deliver your sister's ashes to you myself."

Jane gently carried the box into Karl. "I can hear some scratching around inside. Will you open it and see what's making the noise?" So while she left the room, Karl opened the box and found Bonnie's ashes in a plastic bag with a twist tie on top. Being a kindly gentleman, he filled the rest of the box with bubble wrap, so the ashes were tight. Then he carefully put it all in another box and headed off to the post office to mail the package to Jason.

Here is a case where honesty is *not* the best policy, because when Karl told them the package contained human remains, they said, " Wow! That will cost $50 to mail." People ashes cost more than mailing a box of books! Is it because human remains get extra tender loving care? I don't think so.

Karl and Jane's son owns a box company. He said, "Bring the ashes over, Dad. I'll mail them out for you, and I won't ask you what's in the box." So that's what they did.

Jason called a couple of weeks later to say he'd received his mother's ashes and had put them in a nice urn he'd bought in Hong Kong. The urn was in a window overlooking the ocean, so mom could see him surf.

Then came the kicker. "Oh, by the way," he added. "Will you sell that Jazzi chair mom had. I'd like to buy a head stone for her when I bring her back to Utah some day, and bury her in the family plot in Heber City."

ORGANIZING FOR FINALS

I still like to go to classes and learn new skills now and then, and my most recent acquisition was a class called *House of Order.* I've been driving everyone crazy with my organizing activities. I organized the closets. I organized the kitchen. I even tried organizing the bill paying, but since Bob is the one who pays, he put his foot down and declared, "I don't want everything put in that little girlie desk of yours in the front hall! I want the bills left in the basket by my easy chair so I can be laid back and comfortable when I have to pay them." So I let him have his way....this time.

The next item on my agenda was to organize all of our important documents in a binder that is ready to go in case of an emergency. One of the divisions in the binder was what to do when one of us kicks the bucket. This is a very deep subject. There are birth certificates, death certificates, funerals, plots for burial, and so on. We bought said plots ten years ago, but in checking, it happened that one of us was to be buried on the east side of the street and the other would be buried on the west side. Who ever died first would get to choose, and then we'd buy a very large headstone in the shape of a foot bridge so our ghosts could travel back and forth to visit. Actually, we did have that little problem fixed so now we will rest side by side, and hold ghostly hands.

We invited a mortuary representative over so he could tell us about a prepaid burial plan. He was an older gentleman, about our age, and introduced himself as a *grief counselor.* I began to lose control when he told us how wise we were to plan ahead. "Not wise; this is a class assignment," I thought. He made himself at home at our dining room table and took out several large binders with 8 by 10 glossy pictures. "First of all" he said, "you'll need a nice leak-proof eternal cement vault."

I covered my mouth and snickered. Who cares if it leaks or not? I'm not planning to recycle the contents of the darn thing. I snorted and looked at Bob. He gave me his, "Don't say a word" look, and so I didn't, but I was having a hard time holding it in.

"Then there's the casket," he continued, after Bob gave him a nod. He opened his books and said, "This is our Slumber Collection. They are top of the line"...meaning the most expensive. "They have an inner spring mattress, and soft quilted liners." In spite of all I could do, I began to giggle. Bob shot me a dirty look, but the *counselor* pushed on.

"This collection also has a pillow that lifts up for viewing and lays flat for burial." It was getting worse as tears came to my eyes and my nose was beginning to run. Bob said to me, "Would you like to be excused to get a handkerchief?"

When I brought my red-eyed self back to the table, *Mr. Grief Counselor* was telling Bob that the lid sealed air tight, and the handles on the sides were big enough for the hands of the pall bearers to grasp comfortably. That was all I could take! I stumbled out into the kitchen and fell on the floor, laughing my head off. Bob ushered the poor man and all his Slumber books out of the door, and promised to call him later and tell him of our decision. Then he came into the kitchen and sat on the floor and laughed with me.

When we called the mortuary the next day, we told them that our kids decided to just strap a stick of dynamite to our dead bodies, take us up the mountains and light the fuse. We'd love being part of the mountain ecology. The *grief counselor* hung up on us!